flex

A LEADER'S GUIDE TO

STAYING NIMBLE AND MASTERING

TRANSFORMATIVE CHANGE

IN THE AMERICAN WORKPLACE

RICK GRIMALDI

WILEY

Published by John Wiley & Sons, Inc., Hoboken, New Jersey.
Published simultaneously in Canada.

For general information on our other products and services or for technical support, please contact our Customer Care Department within the United States at (800) 762-2974, outside the United States at (317) 572-3993 or fax (317) 572-4002.

Wiley publishes in a variety of print and electronic formats and by print-on-demand. Some material included with standard print versions of this book may not be included in e-books or in print-on-demand. If this book refers to media such as a CD or DVD that is not included in the version you purchased, you may download this material at http://booksupport.wiley.com. For more information about Wiley products, visit www.wiley.com.

Library of Congress Cataloging-in-Publication Data

Names: Grimaldi, Rick, author.
Title: Flex : a leader's guide to staying nimble and mastering
    transformative change in the American workplace / Rick Grimaldi.
Description: Hoboken, New Jersey : Wiley, [2021] | Includes bibliographical
    references and index.
Identifiers: LCCN 2020053696 (print) | LCCN 2020053697 (ebook) | ISBN
    9781119795100 (hardback) | ISBN 9781119795124 (adobe pdf) | ISBN
    9781119795117 (epub)
Subjects: LCSH: Work environment—United States.
Classification: LCC HD7654 .G775 2021 (print) | LCC HD7654 (ebook) | DDC
    658.3/12—dc23
LC record available at https://lccn.loc.gov/2020053696
LC ebook record available at https://lccn.loc.gov/2020053697

Cover Design and Images: Wiley

SKY10024159_01212021

For Shepard and Beau: the future is yours for the making.

CONTENTS

FOREWORD

Never has it been more essential for leaders and executives to understand the radical shifts that are reshaping work in America today. Only by coming together—inside every single rural and urban community—can we meet this moment to deliver the skills and opportunities we need to step into the future we deserve.

Like me, Rick Grimaldi has studied the world of work throughout his entire career. As former deputy general counsel to Governor Tom Ridge (who later went on to become the first US secretary of Homeland Security) and chief counsel for the Pennsylvania Department of Labor and Industry, he learned how to lead effectively on labor issues, manage disruption in the workplace, and adapt to change.

During his 30 years as a labor lawyer, Rick has managed human relations for a multinational corporation and consulted with dozens and dozens of small, medium, and large companies around the country on how to build a better workforce. His diverse leadership experiences have conferred unusual perspective on the most effective ways to grow profitability, solve workplace challenges, and be an employer of choice . . . even as the pace of change quickens.

As the first African American woman elected to the US House of Representatives from Delaware, I'm particularly aware of how far this country has come in creating a more inclusive culture . . . and how far we still have to go. The business case is compelling.

Now, more than ever, big change requires bold ideas . . . and you'll find them in these pages. As I write this foreword, our country is facing unprecedented challenges that seem poised to shift the paradigm of our future.

A health crisis that is amplifying existing income and racial disparities, long-held institutional inequities that have given rise to racial and social unrest, and an environmental crisis that will shape not only the job market for future generations but also the very planet they will inherit. How well we respond and react to these changes will dictate our success as a nation for decades to come.

From manufacturing to transportation, technology is rapidly remaking entire industries through automation and artificial intelligence. As someone who's always championed college affordability and practical training, I believe it's never been more important to recalibrate American education to available jobs that offer a living wage. Read on to find out how creative educational institutions are doing just that.

Ultimately, as Rick points out, it will be companies that can flex in the face of change that will win the war for talent and be rewarded by the market. Perhaps no event in American history has made this clearer than our recent pandemic.

Will your organization be disrupted? Or will it become a disruptor that thrives for impact and prosperity? Now is the time to be proactive. Fortunately, this is just the guide you need to master change.

—Lisa Blunt Rochester
Cochair, Future of Work Caucus

PREFACE

"What do you do for a living?"

It's one of the very first questions most of us ask in a casual conversation with a new acquaintance. That's because, for most of us, work is at the epicenter of our lives. It informs our identity. Understanding another's métier provides quick insight about someone. After all, work is how we feed our families and fund our dreams.

And if we're very fortunate, it feeds our creativity and sense of purpose and accomplishment in the world. For better or for worse, work is a defining characteristic of our lives.

But here's the thing: The world of work is changing rapidly and in new and unprecedented ways. And that change is occurring faster than ever before. Truths about workers and what they want in a job—things that have seemed self-evident up until now—are just no longer true.

Those who are leading for tomorrow understand this seismic shift. They recognize that their success is predicated on recruiting a skilled workforce as well as their ability to engage and retain those workers in service of the company's goals in the years ahead.

Those who ignore these trends do so at their own peril and will lose the war for talent (and thereby risk their business) in the coming years. Never has it been so urgent to put a finger on the pulse of trends shaping tomorrow's labor force and respond quickly.

We're living in an age when a company's good reputation can fizzle fast with a single viral Facebook post or cringeworthy Glassdoor review. As a labor attorney and employee relations specialist, I've worked with dozens, if not hundreds, of companies that have fought with unions, suffered expensive lawsuits, treated their employees poorly, and lost lucrative business to competitors as a result.

However, I have also been privileged to work with companies that really get it. They recognize the value of calibrating their business to what matters most to employees. They actively work to hire and maintain a diverse workforce. And they are leaning in to experiment with new ways to adapt to the changing needs of the world. The market has rewarded these companies.

Forward-thinking leaders keep close tabs on the many implications of the ever-evolving world of work and reshape their policies and procedures with creative solutions that work for everyone.

That's a mission-critical skill today with the whirlwind of changes remaking the landscape of work. Just consider the stratospheric rise of the gig economy. Is it a good thing for tomorrow's organizations? A bad thing? The gig economy's not going anywhere soon so businesses must understand that the next generation of talent is no longer motivated by "30 years and a watch."

Plus, the advent of new technology is now expanding the economic pie for some even as it unemploys and underemploys others. Assistive technologies are enabling more people with disabilities to join the workforce just as factories are trading out their unskilled workers on the factory floor for college-educated individuals who can run computers. What will this mean for vast populations of workers who can no longer work?

That depends on the commitment and creativity of the companies who employ them. Will you be part of the solution?

INTRODUCTION

The Future is now.

Source: George Allen, Legendary Football Coach.

Recently, my daughter, a newly minted college graduate, kicked off a search for her very first job. She posted her resume on LinkedIn, networked via Facebook, and then submitted scores of applications to online job boards and other internet-based career sites.

After that, those websites scrubbed her application—and those of thousands of applicants just like her—for "key words" to match her with potential employers through an algorithm not unlike Tinder's "match, chat, date" approach to pairing prospective love interests in our disconnected yet wired world.

My daughter and I shared any number of late night conversations about weighty topics related to work. We talked about the arc of a career and the many changes taking place today in the world of work.

And it got me thinking about the quantum leaps I've observed and experienced in my own lifetime immersion in work as I interacted with my bosses and colleagues, conducted business, managed employees, and advised others about how to be good employers.

I've done it all . . . from selling newspapers on the beach to washing pots and pans at restaurants. I've waited tables, saved lives as a summer lifeguard, made change at a pinball arcade, and worked at a water circus. (No, not as an aqua clown.)

I flipped burgers at a Philly cheesesteak joint (practically a rite of passage for Philly kids), served up cocktails with late night advice at a bar, and during my college years, I "candled" eggs during the graveyard shift at an egg processing company to ensure they were safe for shipping to consumers. I pumped gas and worked retail, hawking menswear.

Later, I built my own law firm and served as deputy general counsel to a governor. I managed 200 attorneys in the legal office of a government agency and helped set labor policy for the Commonwealth of Pennsylvania. I shaped human resources policy for a large multinational corporation. And I taught business ethics to community college students (including convicted prisoners at the state penitentiary).

I've even worked as an AM talk radio host while also continuing to practice law for 30 years now, mostly working for employers.

In short, I understand—through considerable personal and professional experience—what it means to be both an employee and an employer. What it means to be a manager of people and be managed by others. I've represented unions and employees as well as small family businesses and huge corporate employers. So I know a bit about the world of work.

As you've no doubt observed through your own work experiences, there are clearly poor places to work and great places to work. There are poor leaders and exceptional leaders. There are truly outstanding employees and, unfortunately, there are also employees who cannot be redeemed.

I've had the privilege over my career to enjoy a close-up view of how each of these dynamics work separately and together in the world of work and what they mean for employees, leaders, and organizations who want to excel in the years to come.

These observations—and the current unprecedented pace of change—have fundamentally shifted the way I view the world of work. And that shift has required me to adapt in ways I never could have imagined when I began my own career.

The reality is that it's foolish and risky for leaders to make assumptions based on what has worked in the past. In forward-thinking organizations, the old "control-manage" model of work has given way to creative collaboration and communication.

We can "rage at the dying of the light," like Welsh poet Dylan Thomas suggests of those who believe they are too old or unwilling to change (or like people concerned about an uncertain fate might do). Or, we can learn to check outdated assumptions when making decisions so we are effective in our efforts to lead profitable, healthy companies into a future that is rapidly reinventing itself. We can learn to *flex*.

This skill set is particularly critical to master in order to respond effectively during pivotal moments inside of an organization. Such moments come in many forms.

For example, the tragic events of 9/11, and then, more recently, COVID-19, created an immediate and profound seismic shift in America's focus on safety and security. Leaders at companies who appreciated the enormity of this shift responded quickly with new policies and targeted training to ensure the workplace remained respectful, healthy, and violence-free.

Downsizings are another moment that occurs frequently inside many companies. The ability to flex is key here also. Managers who can communicate these events organization-wide with sensitivity and transparency fare far better than those who cannot.

Leaders who are skilled at demonstrating compassion and active listening skills are often successful at maintaining the morale of remaining employees while assisting departing employees in letting go of disappointment so they can move forward with a focus on the future.

Competitive threats and societal movements, such as #MeToo, offer make-or-break moments for organizations. Although it's easy to reach out to a lawyer to navigate those moments, I've learned that lawyers tend to zero in on risks from legal issues while often missing the far more important context of the challenge.

The best way to win a lawsuit is to avoid it altogether by cultivating a willingness to take an unflinching look at uncomfortable organizational culture issues, address outdated human resources policies, actively engage all stakeholders, and end the kinds of injustices—financial and otherwise—that give rise to these difficulties. Organizations that embrace those truisms save money, avoid the challenges of unionization, and spend less time in court.

We can spend our energy and resources working to shut out change that is uncomfortable, inconvenient, and, frankly, inevitable. But it's a useless endeavor in my experience. That path leads to irrelevancy. There are plenty of others happy to take our jobs and customers.

Instead, let's be nimble as we lean into change to proactively shape responsive organizations that value creativity and innovation to foster success. Today, more than ever, we need to care about relationships and be prepared for the disruptions that will inevitably come.

As someone who's been fortunate to have a front-row seat during the onslaught of mega and micro influences reshaping work in America today, I invite you to consider the ways in which successful companies not only navigate unimaginable disruption but also embrace it as an opportunity to learn and grow.

1 The World Is Changing

Change is the law of life. And those who look only to the past or present are certain to miss the future.

Source: John F. Kennedy Address in the Assembly Hall at the Paulskirche in Frankfurt (266), June 25, 1963, Public Papers of the Presidents: John F. Kennedy, 1963.

It's certainly no surprise that the world is changing, right? Progress and innovation have always been the natural order of things.

Hunter-gatherers evolved into an agrarian society focused on farming. Much later, America's industrial economy gave way to a postindustrial society, transitioning from a society that primarily provided manufactured goods to one that provides services.

Plus, world events—wars, natural disasters, political leaders, plagues, and viruses—have all delivered tsunamis of change since the beginning of time.

But here's what is new and radical in the world we live in today: the frenetic *pace* of change. That is unprecedented in the history of the world. The period with which change occurs has become radically *compressed*.

And that is having a profound effect on the world of work. There's a cognitive dissonance—a sort of psychological stress experienced worldwide—as we collectively struggle to match our behaviors, decisions, and expectations to a world that is evolving at warp speed. And all of these changes are rushing into a work environment that seems forever in flux.

Where is all this change coming from? It's due to a set of complex and ever-mutating trends both internal and external to our society. And together, they are creating a perfect storm of chaos with grave implications for businesses and companies that don't recognize and respond.

Let's consider them one at a time.

The Face of America Is Changing

One of the biggest changes sweeping our nation is the pace of diversity. The percentage of white Americans is shrinking. In fact, by the year 2045, the census projects that whites will make up just under half of the US population, officially making them a minority. America will also be almost one-quarter Hispanic and nearly 8% Asian.[1]

Where will US population growth come from exactly? International migration. As the largely white population retires, it will be youthful minorities who take their place. By 2060, the census estimates that only 36% of those under 18 will be white. Non-whites already make up the majority of newborns and kids in K–12 schools in the US today.

The political schism in America today makes sense in this context, doesn't it? The on-the-ground realities are quite different for the declining white population and the emerging multiracial population. As America rapidly becomes more ethnically diverse, companies will need to recognize resistance to change among the ranks, become adept at fostering acceptance and inclusion, and actively work to effectively engage a diverse workforce.

Paying lip service to "diversity initiatives" will brand organizations as out-of-step, making it more challenging to recruit talent. As you will learn, what really matters instead is consistent hiring practices that actually reflect an inclusive and diverse workforce.

When a potential hire looks around the office or the plant, what are they noting about your organization? Is the executive team elderly, male, and white? Or does it accurately reflect the diverse racial and gender makeup that is their reality? Here's a tantalizing stat to consider: in 2019, 60% of companies in the US did not have a *single* woman on the board.[2]

Also, senior citizens are soon expected to outnumber children for the first time in our history. In just one decade from now—by 2030—every baby boomer will be at least 65 years old, ushering in a radical new era of slower population growth.[3] In fact, by 2060, there will be just 2.5 workers (down from 3.5 workers) to drive the economy for every retired individual.[4]

Millennials Are Taking Over

Recently, millennials surpassed Gen Xers as the largest generation of workers.[5] And that trend has plenty of critical implications as well. Just as America is experiencing a widening gap between whites and non-whites, so, too, is it struggling with a schism between the experience of older Americans and millennials.

Millennials are early adopters of technology. Unlike their older peers, they've grown up with the internet in a connected society replete with social media and other online solutions oriented platforms. Technology solutions are intuitive for them.

At first glance, it might seem millennials have a societal advantage due to their facility with technology compared to older generations.

But, although they may find it easier to navigate the latest app or trending technology, they are also less at ease with real-time communication than older Americans. This is true in the workplace as well. In other words, even as they are more connected, they are also more *dis*connected.

Millennials are struggling in other ways, too. The American Dream they've watched their parents embrace is fading from view. It seems unattainable for millennials as they struggle under the burden of historic loan debt, soaring health care costs, and flattened wages, forcing many to live at home well into their 30s.

Sets of couples are sharing tiny apartments in large urban cities with runaway housing costs and forgoing consumer purchases such as new cars that previous generations took for granted as a normal perk of life after college. Millennials are realizing that, for the first time in history, they are unlikely to do as well as their parents have done.

Will those resentments play out in unforeseen ways as they ultimately arrive in the C suite and must allocate financial resources for older generations? If not millennials, who will drive the economic engine as baby boomers retire and reduce spending?

Ultimately, it's in the workplace (as well as society at large) where these generational trends often work at cross-purposes when workers' values and communication styles conflict. Successful companies will be those who can flex and find creative ways to harness the diverse strengths of their employees in service of the company's goals.

Education Isn't Training for Reality

How exactly will we prepare and train students for this new and ever-shifting work landscape? Unfortunately, our nation's educational systems are training for a reality that no longer exists. Teaching is outmoded.

Education also must change to respond to the changes in American demographics we've been discussing. Universities are combatting declining enrollment trends, which causes a cascade of consequences reshaping American education.

Why is college enrollment down? In part, because the national birth rate is down: 20% since the 2008 recession,[6] actually. For millennials, it's not just a question of how to afford a home and a new car; this generation has no idea how they will pay for health care and childcare, much less a college education for their progeny.

In short, they can't afford to have kids. That's a big reason why fertility rates are at a record low. And if we look forward 18 years from that decision to forgo a pregnancy, we can expect to see a major decline in college admissions beginning in around 2026.[7]

It's not surprising, right? Fewer babies means fewer college freshman. But how will universities fill their enrollment quotas when their financial model is under stress? Perhaps with an increasing number of international students as many do now?

These kinds of demographic trends are already putting education on a collision course with the future as we know it. Traditional college markets—such as white students from economically privileged families in the Northeast—are being replaced by an increase in Hispanics in the Southwest who, for a variety of reasons, may be less sold on the value of a college education.[8]

For many white students from middle- and upper-class families, college has always been an important steppingstone to an enriching career or well-paying job. But the Hispanic college market is far softer. These students are less likely to enroll in a selective college in the first place, and if they do enroll at all, for a variety of reasons, they are less likely to attend full-time.[9]

Another reason there are fewer students heading to college: there are fewer kids graduating from high school. Illiteracy is becoming an increasing problem. In urban areas, where students frequently struggle with poverty and food security, a high school degree doesn't seem that compelling when it's easier to get a job in retail in order to earn money to live. So it may not surprise you to learn that forecasts suggest an 11% decrease in first-time college goers by the end of the 2020s.[10]

You might think universities would respond to this declining market by cutting prices, but that seems unlikely given that reducing revenue doesn't offer a net economic gain to compensate for fewer students. And here's another thing to consider as we wonder what the future of education will look like: how important *is* it to be a college graduate to succeed in tomorrow's workforce?

And if it's important, is a two-year community college degree enough? What's the best return on investment for students based on the considerable expense of an American college degree?

The answer to each of those questions is that it depends on where you live and what you want to do. It also depends on the ability of forward-thinking educational institutions to anticipate the needs of specific skill sets in local industries that are reinventing themselves again and again as new technologies accelerate the way they do business so they create true value for their students. In short, college as we know it is under tremendous pressure to flex.

For parents who are still hoping to send their student to college, the value proposition has changed, too. When they consider taking out a second mortgage on their home so their student can attend a top-tier university, they want to know that their child will be employable in a competitive industry. They want to know that university will graduate their child in four years instead of six because space in required courses is available.

Nontraditional students who do decide to pursue a college degree want to know that they are partnering with an educational institution that understands the challenges they face to make it to class every day. Many are juggling work commitments, a lengthy commute, or caregiving for parents to make their dream of a college degree a reality. They are hunting for flexibility.

In the same way, what will happen to blue-collar workers who have spent 30 years on the floor of a manufacturing facility doing unskilled work when the company retools into a high-tech environment? Will they face layoffs and be replaced with new college grads with an information technology degree?

Nontraditional students—older students considering retraining and younger students not completely sold on college—have no interest in a "well-rounded liberal arts degree." Rather, they want to know there's a good return on investment for an actual employable skill set in exchange for their hard-earned dollars.

For just this reason, many nontraditional—and other—students will turn away from elite universities that seem out of touch in favor of pursuing online options or a degree from a trade school

There are 30 million jobs in America today that pay an average of $50,000 per year that don't require a degree from a four-year university. Despite the benefits and pensions these jobs offer, there's still a shortage of workers trained in such vocational schools.[11]

And it's the same situation when it comes to community college.

In the past, students and their parents saw them as a steppingstone into a four-year university. But expect them to take a more central role in creative partnering with local employers in the years to come.

So, yes, education simply must reinvent itself at every level—from K to 12 and prestigious colleges to trade schools and community colleges—to keep pace with the needs of students, the needs of employers, and the needs of society itself. No longer can we allow urban inner-city schools to decay leaving impoverished students ill-equipped to meet the needs of employers in their communities. We need them.

Language Is Changing: R U Up to Speed?

Not only are demographics and education changing but also the way we communicate is changing. Much like cells in biological evolution, which are constantly mutating according to their environment, so too is language ever evolving.

Linguists study this phenomenon,[12] in fact, and talk about the concept of "drift," the seeming random nature of how language changes over time, much like the concept of genetic drift in biology, which studies how existing genes vary in a population with random sampling. The idea here is that, whether we are talking about genes or language, you can study whether (and how) it survives and reproduces in the future.

When it comes to evolving language, it's typically a result of certain pressures that come to bear. Changing social norms, for example, signal which words are socially acceptable or not. Then there are technical innovations that make it more convenient to communicate within certain parameters.

Sometimes it's just the way that some verb conjugations are harder to remember than others, making some words used far less frequently until they fall out of our lexicon. When it comes to other words, they become favored by "insiders" or "outsiders" or are only used by those in power (such as corporate executives)—or those who feel disenfranchised (such as protesters).

As our world reshapes itself through changes in generational and racial demographics, the language we use—the way we communicate—is reshaping itself in some important ways. And it's critical to be aware and adept at navigating this change in the American workplace.

Communication Is Faster . . . For Better or for Worse

Humans have, of course, have been communicating over millennia. What's new, as we've just discussed, is the pace of change today with respect to language and communication.

Way back in 130,000 BCE, early people shared their experiences and documented primitive life via cave paintings through pigments made from fruit and berry juice.

Much later, about 1440, human communication took a giant leap forward with the invention of the Gutenberg printing press in France, giving rise to books and other written communication, while effectively standardizing spelling and punctuation.

As literacy grew, it became possible to pen a letter to a loved one and have it delivered by stagecoach and later by mail courier. In the 20th century, radio, newspapers, and television drove more innovation in language.

But think again about the pace of these innovations. Just 40 years ago—before the use of email became widespread in the 1990s—we expected to wait five days for a letter to reach someone across the country. Unless, of course, we paid for expedited delivery through FedEx or a similar service.

Xerox introduced fax machines as early as 1964, but they didn't really take off in corporate America until the late 1980s. And, although plenty of companies still use them, many are increasingly using

Cloud-based fax services, which create images or PDF files to be sent over email. (And thank goodness for that. Nobody wants to sort through the pile of faxes on slippery paper at the office looking for the missing page as we once did.)

But the internet has changed all that. It's sped up communication even as it has forgone the importance of syntax in favor of a return to character-based communication. It is hard to ignore the irony of thousands of years of advances from cave paintings as a form of written communication to the use of the emoji today.

Although it's true that language has always been dynamic, with colloquialisms going in and out of vogue, this development is revolutionary throughout history. Texting means that you will receive a communication instantaneously with an instantaneous response expected.

So we've moved from books on a printing press to television to fax to email to texts . . . condensing the time frame of communication from years to weeks to days to immediately. And that is changing the world of work in some pretty surprising and unintentional ways.

One unfortunate side effect of the texting revolution—when texting is primary and email is a back-up communication solution—is that expectations of response time have ratcheted up alarmingly.

It's not uncommon for attorneys I know to get seven texts from a client or a colleague in a single hour they spend in a meeting or on a conference call. When those seven texts aren't answered within that 60-minute time frame, an email follow-up will arrive soon afterwards asking, "Did you get my text?"

As harried workers try to respond by text, email, and phone (while attending a videoconference on their watch), this has repercussions for the degree to which we are offering useful ideas with our divided focus at meetings or with clients.

If you're working on a complex task or trying to thoughtfully solve a difficult dilemma, you will likely be repeatedly interrupted by everyone from your spouse wanting to make dinner plans and the plumber you're trying to schedule, to clients and coworkers. The fact is: it's no longer okay to be "unreachable."

One the one hand, the rapid pace of communication is a wonderful thing. In the face of globalization, it's made the world smaller. Our abbreviated texts and single-line emails are frequently an efficient and useful response to globalization in a busy world.

On the other hand, this phenomenon contributes to a conflict-avoidant culture. Just think about the "ghosting" phenomenon on the rise today, when millennials signal their disinterest in a friend or new love interest by essentially *ignoring* the text. It contributes to social disconnection that is bleeding into the workforce. How ironic that so much "connectivity" in our modern era is actually leading to less connection in real life.

The Rise of Social Media

First there was America Online or AOL (Are you old enough to remember the sound of the modem connecting when you logged on?), which seeded our universal addiction to internet connectivity with the beginning of Yahoo's online chat forums and early email.

This was followed in the early 2000s by a bevy of websites ratcheting up our connectivity and taking social media from a nerdy techno-babbling hobby into mainstream daily communication for most of us. There was Friendster (for making friends, obviously), Classmates.com (for alumni), LinkedIn (for work contacts), and Myspace, the social precursor to Facebook.

Today, Facebook, which was originally concepted for networking among college students. has grown into a prolific and widely used social media network with 1.3 billion active users since it debuted in 2006. Then, of course, there is also Twitter, Instagram, Snapchat, Vine, and Google+ with their own unique value propositions for users. TikTok, a video-sharing network, has also recently joined the ranks.

This has all resulted in a barrage of emoji use by all. Cute icons that are angry, teary, anxious, and laughing are everywhere in our communications today.

What you may not be aware of, though, is that how we communicate—and whether we are comfortable with this type of common shorthand at work—determines the degree to which we remain relevant and valued at work.

Science Fiction Can't Keep Up

Of all the ways the world is changing faster than ever, technology may be one of the most striking trends to consider. Aside from social media, it's had an oversized impact on virtually (pun intended) everything we do.

Just consider the rise of Apple. On January 9, 2007, Steve Jobs took to the stage and introduced the iPhone: Apple's vision for the modern cell phone. The device sported a large touchscreen, featured a simple, easy-to-navigate interface, and placed the internet and a camera into the pocket of consumers worldwide.

The industry was ripe for disruption because the market was dominated by "clam-shell" phones that were not optimized for the creation or consumption of media or browsing the internet. Although some manufacturers produced cell phones that could be used for these purposes, they relied on small screens, physical keyboards, unreliable trackballs, and low-resolution cameras. This all changed the moment Jobs walked up on the stage.

In the years following the iPhone's unveiling, the smartphone industry's response to Apple was nothing short of breathtaking. Smartphone manufacturers, including electronic behemoth Samsung, released a flurry of new devices to combat the iPhone's prowess . . . delivering innovative new features such as wireless charging, curved screens, mobile payment options, and improved photography. Other companies, such as Google, were also spurred to create their own smartphone operating systems and larger technological ecosystems.

In Ireland alone, where Apple's European headquarters is located, iPhone exports were responsible for *one-quarter* of the country's economic growth.

In South Korea, exports of semiconductors (a key component in smartphone production) accounted for 17.1% of all of the country's exports. As you can see, smartphone innovation has benefited far more than just consumers. Rather, it's been an engine of economic growth worldwide. And that's just one example of technology reshaping our world, including the world of work.

Recently, I had a conversation with an Uber driver—a ride-sharing concept that itself was brand new just a decade ago—about the impact of Google Maps on his job. He was animated as we discussed the "flying taxis" currently under development by companies like Tesla that are leading a revolution in alternative energy.

"Think about it," he said. "I couldn't do this job with a paper map. Not only that, but I'm pretty sure Uber wouldn't even exist today without Google Maps." He's speaking, of course, about the importance of GPS, the global positioning system. Thanks to satellites in space that ping our location, we navigate even the remotest areas on the planet with ease.

And this has given rise to the gig economy that is Uber, Lyft, and other ridesharing services and changing the way consumers buy and companies sell goods. Is the gig economy a good thing or a bad thing? Does the flexibility that drivers can make their own part-time hours offset the depreciation on their car and lack of health benefits? We will examine this and other aspects of the gig economy in Chapter 4.

A Dystopian Reality

Way back in 1968, on the popular sci-fi television series *Star Trek,* Scotty leaned into his hand console and asked, "Computer, what is the distance between Earth and the Romulan galaxy?" It seemed fantastical at the time . . . that a computer could instantly deliver that information.

Was he speaking to Siri even back then? Now that students worldwide have been schooled via Zoom, it's easier than ever to imagine a student today working with a partner who is an actual computer, perhaps creating a virtual model of that Romulan galaxy and then sending it to a 3D printer to produce an immediate 3D model of it.

What was once science fiction is now just a Siri request away. Artificial intelligence is here. Indeed, 21st-century technology has become embedded in our daily lives as an indispensable part of how we work and play.

The proliferation of apps—everything from meditation and rain sounds while we sleep to Cloud-based task organizing and expense capturing—are available to us for instant download for just $3.99 (as long as you don't mind uploading your credit card data . . . a prospect that was unthinkable just a few decades ago).

That's made possible by the seamless interface with the two major mobile operating systems (Android and iOS) on which much of the world's population depends.[13]

What's more, the Internet of Things has now arrived and is innovating rapidly. What is the Internet of Things, exactly? It's a term describing the billions of physical devices connected to the internet. Each device is equipped to sensors to tune into the ambient environment. And every single one is collecting and sharing your data.

The Internet of Things includes items as small as a tiny pill that can diagnose clinical information on patients who swallow it and as large as driverless cars and trucks with trailers. Think smart watches that record your daily steps and grade your fitness. Or the heat in your home that switches on automatically when you enter.

Technology is remaking our world dramatically with everything from brain implants restoring movement in paralyzed patients with spinal cord injuries to gene therapy 2.0, which is curing rare disorders and readying to take on rampant killers such as cancer and heart disease and deadly viruses such as COVID-19.

Meanwhile, in Europe and Asia, governments are using face-detecting systems to authorize payments and stop criminals in their tracks.[14] Stay tuned to see if this new trend catches on worldwide.

It's Getting Hotter

You'd have to be living under a rock in 2020 if you've missed the global discussion on our earth's changing climate. And, although many still want to debate whether these represent normal fluctuations in warming, as Swedish-born activist Greta Thunberg says, "Don't listen to me; listen to the scientists."

It's undeniable that summers will grow longer, wildfires will become more common, and sea levels will continue to rise. In the United States specifically, climate forecasters anticipate shorter winters and longer summers in the Northeast with a decline in species that support important fisheries. They expect higher health risks due to food from contaminated waters in New England's rivers, canals, and coasts.[15]

More than half of major cities in the Southeast are experiencing worsening heat waves. In the Midwest, a rise in climate-related ground-level ozone is expected to cause an avalanche of premature deaths. Expect more lung disease and higher rates of illness for the elderly, too. More than a quarter of US agriculture comes from this region, but the higher temperatures will likely also mean declining crop yields.[16]

Droughts and wildfires in California and the Southwest means forests there are emitting more carbon into the atmosphere than they used. And these greenhouse gas emissions predict a tripling of the number of large wildfires. Meanwhile, ocean waters will warm California coastal waters between 4°F and 7°F by 2100.

In the Northwest, these greenhouse gas emissions will likely cause winter warming, decimating fish populations and closing fisheries. Mountain snowpacks will melt increasing wildfires. Alaska is actually warming faster than any other state.[17]

And so it goes. On and on. What does it all mean?

Aside from the very real and imminent toll that these conditions will have on humans as a species, the effect of climate change on the business world is potentially immeasurable. And yet, emissions fell in China by 25% with the COVID-19 lockdown there. Pollution in New York City was down by 50% due to its containment measures.[18]

Is it possible the world can rally long term, as it seemingly did during the pandemic, when threats feel less urgent? Even if we somehow come together soon as one people to address our carbon emissions effectively—to stop or reverse climate change—it's undeniable that much damage has already been done. Sea levels will continue to rise, which will crowd out the populations in low-lying areas that will flood.

But aside from fundamentally changing the way we live, climate change will also change how we do business and engage in commerce. Just as COVID-19 brought once unthinkable new realities to daily life—such as mask wearing in public and possibly the end of the hand shake—so, too, will climate change affect the energy we use, the materials we build with, and how we invest. It will also give rise to new industries and ultimately a green economy . . . all important ways that the world of work is changing.

As blogger and technology evangelist Robert Scoble once noted, "Change is inevitable, and the disruption it causes often brings both inconvenience and opportunity."[19] As you will see, history is replete with organizations that failed to see change as a chance to evolve. It's also full of visionary organizations that fought back their fears to seize new opportunity.

Those who continue to do business as usual despite the storm of change will become disrupted. They will fade into obscurity as savvy new organizations—disruptors—take their place . . . winning over the customers and employees of those other companies with a responsive new approach to the world around them.

Companies that flex *own* the future, as you will see.

Key Learning Points

1. The current pace of change is unprecedented in the history of the world. That's creating a pressure-cooker environment in the American workplace.

2. Minority populations are rapidly taking the place of the Caucasian majority of the past. Plus, millennials are taking over. Successful organizations will use inclusive hiring and engagement practices or lose the war on talent if they provide only lip service to diversity initiatives instead.

3. Our system of education is out of step with the ways the world of work is changing and so is not meeting critical needs of employers for skilled workers. K–12, high school, college, and vocational training must undergo a radical shift to keep America competitive in the global marketplace.

4. The way we communicate is changing due to both generational preferences and technological innovation. Misaligned communications are resulting in a dangerously conflict-avoidant work culture.

5. Climate change will change how we do business, and affect energy use, building materials, and how we invest. Ultimately, it will drive the adoption of a green economy and, perhaps, global cooperation.

2 America Was Built on Change

We are not makers of history. We are made by history.

Source: Martin Luther King, I Have a Dream, 1968.

© The Estate of Martin Luther King, Jr.

So how did we get here? It wasn't so long ago, in post-industrial America, that the GI bill delivered on the American Dream. With free college tuition and low-interest mortgages for World War II veterans, the promise of prosperity was tangible.

What did that look like in 1950? A youthful New Yorker—we'll call him John Young—nabbed a job right out of college, put on a flannel suit, and commuted to work at a swank Manhattan ad company. Eventually, John likely made partner as a result of his hard work and loyalty to the firm. And, after 30 years or so, he eventually retired, somewhere between the ages of 60 and 65.

Even those who didn't head to college were successful in those days. John's cousin in Philly—let's call him Joe—jumped on the El and commuted to the Old Nabisco plant on Roosevelt Boulevard in the northeast section of the city. Joe was in maintenance, belonged to the union, and made a living wage. He was able to take his family to the Jersey shore for a week every summer.

And on that salary, Joe likely saved enough money to retire right there at the shore: living on a company pension, a monthly Social Security check, and a bit of his savings. In fact, Joe enjoyed the same benefits of being solidly middle class as his better-educated cousin, John. In those days, if you were willing to put in the time and work hard, you'd be rewarded in America.

Today, the notion of working for a single employer—or even several of them—over a lifetime seems, frankly, quaint. Pensions have long since evaporated for most Americans. When it comes to saving for retirement, we're on our own . . . even as many of us juggle several jobs or work in the gig economy to either make ends meet now or fund that passion project for the future, if possible.

So what has changed, exactly? And what does it all mean for employers and employees today?

Flex or Be Disrupted

If there's a lesson we can take from history, it's that disruption is inevitable. Huge shifts in how business is done have always reshaped the world of work. In the face of those major shifts, however, some companies have thrived and others have atrophied and been replaced by more savvy competitors.

Some leaders have tried to tune out change in favor of business as usual in the face of monumental change, and others have sought out and seized new opportunities. In short, some companies were disrupted and others flexed and became the disruptors.

To truly grasp the seismic shifts underway in the world of work today, we'll need to first consider how work has already changed. By understanding some of the disruptive influences, legislation, and socioeconomic forces that have shaped the changing world of work throughout American history, we can better assess where we are headed next.

So let's take a whirlwind tour of the changing world of work in the United States over the last 200 or so years.

Getting by in Preindustrial America

Work has always been the way in which we have provided for ourselves: shelter, food, and childcare. In fact, how we work—along with the ability to communicate and use tools—has been a differentiator between humans and other species.[1]

Before the advent of the Industrial Revolution, which began in the mid-1700s, America looked very different. It was an agrarian society.

In other words, men like John in New York City were likely farmers instead of ad men. Joe from Philly probably worked as a blacksmith to shoe horses for his community in those days.

During this period, most work activity existed at a subsistence level. The primary goal of work was to provide for the immediate needs of ones' family: sewing the clothing the children would wear or growing enough vegetables to serve at dinner rather than to sell to others in a marketplace.[2]

There were some, of course, who sold their goods—seamstresses selling clothing to neighbors or blacksmiths selling horseshoes out of their barn—but these tiny operations were a far cry from the behemoth manufacturing and factory operations that arrived after the Industrial Revolution. Instead, "enterprises" consisted of individual workers working out of their homes.[3]

As you might anticipate, work tasks on family farms in agrarian society were divided up according to gender norms. Men tilled the soil and harvested, women watched the kids, cooked the meals, and sewed clothes. Think of it as early apprenticeship for sons and daughters (but mostly sons).[4]

And who performed the bulk of the field labor during this period in history? It should come as no surprise: indentured slaves did. Nearly 4 million of them[5] who were born or forced into bondage.

Until the advent of the Civil War and President Abraham Lincoln's Emancipation Proclamation in January 1863, the antebellum South was particularly a slave society. Plantation owners in Virginia and Maryland profited off of labor-intensive tobacco crops while South Carolina exported rice and indigo, and other southern states used slave labor to profit from the cotton industry.

The Assembly Line Changed Everything

Beginning first in Great Britain, the Industrial Revolution spread, over time, to America in the mid-19th century as machines and manufacturing ratcheted up production in the chemical, iron, and water power industries. Meanwhile, the textile industry led the way as the dominant industry for employment.[6]

If we wanted to characterize the huge shift in work during the Industrial Revolution into a single idea, it might be this: America overwhelmingly swapped out hand tools for power tools, resulting in major economic and social reorganization.

Woodworking lathes that had endured for centuries were replaced by industrial machine tools. And because they were far more precise, large numbers of identical parts could be produced cost-effectively with fewer workers, an innovation useful in many industries. In fact, this production system—many finished identical parts—came to be known as the "American System."[7]

In reality, systems of mass production were first developed in France, Britain, and Sweden. For example, it was actually a French engineer, Marc Brunel, who first invented a system for producing wooden pulley blocks, replacing the need for 100 men with just 10 to produce 160,000 pulley blocks per year. Now that's innovation!

And yet, the British largely ignored Brunel's achievements until the late 19th century when they saw how Americans had adapted and matured early European ideas like his to mass produce clocks, sewing machines, textile machines, and small arms, among other items. And that's perhaps why it is actually Eli Whitney, best known for his invention of the cotton gin, who is credited with the development of the American system.[8]

Daily life for most Americans was transformed by these innovations. For one thing, work shifted away from the home to the factory. Instead of accomplishing a work goal together—as they had during harvest time—families became more fragmented. Men trudged off to the factory, and women and children stayed home and actually contributed *less* to work outside the home than they had in preindustrial America.

Another impact of the shift of work to the factory was the loss of flexibility for work. Instead of farmers acting as their own boss, deciding when to knock off early for fishing and when to work past dinner and dark to maximize the harvest, employers now set the hours.[9] And yet, despite some of these drawbacks, America's population grew steadily and the standard of living flourished across the nation.

It was all thanks to the widespread use of the assembly line. If you're like many, it's probably the visual that comes most quickly to mind when someone mentions the Industrial Revolution.

Where did it come from? We can trace the assembly line back to the machine trolley systems of 19th century meatpacking plants in the American Midwest. The trolleys were located just overhead workers who were stationary. Then, as the machine moved meat carcasses overhead, each worker performed just a single task that the machine dictated, which dramatically improved productivity.[10]

It wasn't long before the efficiency of these early assembly lines caught the notice of one particular individual who would go on to revolutionize the American factory and, as a result, fundamentally change the economic future of America.

Enter Henry Ford.

The Ultimate Disruptor

In his early years, Ford built racing cars. But he harbored a radical dream: to build a car for every man. Nearly 100 years before Steve Jobs delighted customers worldwide with smartphones they didn't know they needed, Henry Ford was the first to design a car for the common person instead of the very wealthy.

Ford was also perhaps the first to meet this goal by reengineering a product in ways that many successful companies have since emulated. (Look no further than the Japanese electronics industry in the 1980s. They outcompeted everyone worldwide through lower product prices using this very approach.)

Here's what Ford did: first, he crystalized his vision of a Model T for the average Joe. Ford's actual words were: "I will build a motor car for the great masses . . . constructed of the best men to be hired, after the simplest designs that modern engineering can devise . . . so low in price that no man making a good salary will be unable to want one—and enjoy with family the blessing of hours of pleasure in God's great open spaces."[11]

In 1905, the average annual household income in America was $500,[12] but the average cost of a car was $1,200, well out of reach for most. So Ford determined that he would slash that cost, introducing his Model T at $825 in 1909 and dropping that price within six years to just $390 when the assembly line allowed him to fully scale up production in 1915.

An important key to that process was to begin by setting the price point for the product *first,* rather than *last.* Instead of adding up the costs and then figuring out what kind of profit he could build in, he determined what the selling point of the automobile must be such that most consumers could afford to buy one.

Ford said success wasn't just about getting economies of scale, but rather the way to engineer and design a product was to work *backwards* from the price. Does that seem a little radical? To just decide on a price without first figuring the actual costs into the equation?

Well, it depends on your goal. Ford's goal was to use the Model T to create a true consumer market and, ultimately, an industrial middle class in America. To spark massive sales, the Model T had to be affordable. So, it was important to work backwards from the final price point.

To achieve that, he anticipated some important economic principles that Ronald Coase, a British Nobel–winning economist and University of Chicago professor, would actually articulate in a scholarly writing a couple of decades later. (Sadly, Coase has been largely forgotten by history.)

In his landmark essay, "The Nature of the Firm,"[13] published way back in 1937, Coase laid out his radical argument for why companies form in the first place: because they can afford to absorb so-called transaction costs.

"The idea behind transaction costs is that there is a lot of overhead required to find the right employee, train them, and negotiate appropriate labor rates and benefits," explains Professor Alexander Cocron, lecturer at Johns Hopkins University's Center for Leadership Education, who has studied Coase's work.

"Plus, someone will need to police that employee to make sure they adhere to their part of the employment bargain. There are negotiations and compensation issues. Those are all expenses—transaction costs—that a company can better absorb through efficiencies and scale than two parties who are contracting directly for a product or service."[14]

In his seminal paper, Coase argued that the optimal size of a company is one in which the internal and external resources provide an optimal balance to absorb transaction costs while not increasing overhead costs so much that an entrepreneur could outcompete them, something that's happening with increasing frequency in today's gig economy.

In other words, Henry Ford figured out that the best way to own the market for American automobiles was to reduce transaction costs for a competitive advantage. In his words: "The reduction of price comes first. We have never considered any costs as fixed. Therefore, we first reduce the price to a point where we believe more sales will result. Then we go ahead and try to make the price. We do not bother about the costs. The new price forces the costs down."[15]

And that's where the assembly line helped a great deal. Using an assembly line shaved 15 minutes off the time it took to manufacture Ford's magneto flywheels, delivering substantial savings on labor. Then he went about using the same approach to radically cut labor time for the chassis, where they reduced the time from six man-hours to just 93 minutes.[16]

Then Ford went even further. As his assembly line became fast and efficient, he could no longer afford to risk interruption of raw materials or components inflows. So he decided to integrate upstream production of his River Rouge Factory, taking all those raw production materials in-house, rather than counting on potentially unreliable third-party organizations (Ultimately, he owned his own glass works, rubber plants, and steel mill!).

With a marketing slogan of "Sunday is for church but Saturday is for driving your Model T," Ford upended or disrupted popular thinking that cars were for rich people only. Ultimately, competitors and parts suppliers were forced to imitate his approach by finding cheaper ways to stay competitive. They, too, swapped out skilled labor with cheaper unskilled labor courtesy of America's rapidly burgeoning factory assembly lines.

Ford's disruptive impulses didn't stop there, either. In a quest to create an industrial middle class—and, let's be honest, to reduce his sky-high employee turnover—he even doubled the hourly wage he was paying his workforce. Factory work was difficult and unrewarding so something had to give.

Ford also played a big role in the push for a weekend away from work. Although the federal government didn't officially enact the 40-hour work week until 1938—and some might credit that to collective bargaining by unions—Ford Motor Co. was giving *their* workers two days off decades before.

The Rise of Organized Labor

As America's industrial economy matured, more women and children moved into the workforce in American factories. Post–Civil War, in the late 19th century, immigrants also arrived from Europe, Asia, and Mexico, all keen to try their hand at the American Dream as the country's economic engine roared ahead with the expansion of big business. Despite the bad rap that immigrants have always gotten in politics, including modern American politics, they were then—and remain now—indispensable to the boom in this country's growth.[17]

However, it would still be more than 50 years before the 40-hour work week was legalized. As business disrupted family farms and workers toiled long hours, conflict began to brew between employers and employees. Workers wanted better hours and safer conditions. They wanted health benefits, assistance to those who were sick or retired, and an end to the practice of child labor.

And that's when the organized labor movement—a major disruptor for businesses both then and now—was born. The idea of the labor union was inspired by ideals from the American Revolution that "fostered social equality, celebrated honest labor, and relied on an independent, virtuous citizenship."[18] A number of early reform movements sprouted up during the 19th century to advocate on behalf of common workers, including the National Labor Union in 1866.

Tensions were high during this time between employers and those who worked for them, leading to plenty of violent strikes. Union leaders were frequently arrested . . . or worse. Businesses fought viciously against workers' efforts to organize.

But actually, the idea behind the National Labor Union was to protect both the rights of employees and employers. The organization encouraged the practice of collective bargaining and put an end to other practices that could harm workers and the American economy.[19]

Sweatshops that had taken advantage of round-the-clock cheap labor sources gave way to standardized hours and minimum wages, eventually completely reshaping the American workforce. But still, the fact remained that there were no real enforceable legal protections in place for workers.

The Great Depression Rocks the Workforce

In the 20th century, a pair of major events took the world of work in America on yet another rollercoaster ride. When the stock market tumbled in 1929, it set off the Great Depression, plummeting industrial output. Consumer spending screeched to a halt and businesses shuttered at a frantic pace. The shockwaves of the Great Depression seemed to threaten the very idea of the long-term viability of capitalism.

As businesses struggled to survive, workers were let go without notice, throwing the lack of legal protections for those workers into stark relief. There was no unemployment compensation or Social Security to fall back on in those days.

In the end, it was government intervention that would turn the tide. When Franklin D. Roosevelt was inaugurated as president in 1933, he stepped in to put people back to work and jumpstarted the American economy with an alphabet soup of New Deal governmental programs.

There was the Works Progress Administration (WPA), a program to put unskilled American men to work on public-private partnerships such as the construction of buildings and roads. The Civilian Conservation Corps (CCC) offered conservation work to young, unmarried men. The Social Security Act (SSA) made direct payments to the elderly while also establishing insurance against unemployment. The Fair Labor Standards Act (FLSA) created the modern minimum wage and standardized hours.

Of particular significance was FDR's establishment of the National Labor Relations Act (NLRA), designed to protect the fragile ecosystem of America's economy. He recognized that the violence of labor clashes could have a devastating effect on the economy finally beginning to sputter to life. (He understood that it was labor *peace* that was called for to kindle the country's prosperity, for both business and workers.)

The NLRA, like the Civil Rights Act that arrived some 30 years later, changed business in huge and unforeseen ways. The act, along with the federal agency created to enforce it, safeguarded employees' rights to collective bargaining and curtailed certain private sector labor and management practices that could harm the general welfare of workers, businesses, and the US economy.[20] Rarely throughout history has such an avalanche of legislation created so much disruption, fundamentally altering the way Americans worked and how American business conducted itself in the marketplace.

After the AFL-CIO was formed, post–World War II, collective bargaining on behalf of workers began to deliver impressive gains for workers, tripling weekly wages in manufacturing; offering unprecedented security against illness, unemployment, and old age through better contracts; and ensuring that employers treated workers fairly.[21] This would be the high-water mark for organized labor because roughly 35% of the nation's private sector workforce (not including agriculture) was unionized during this period.[22]

Because of all these improvements, many today still credit organized labor with the creation of the middle class in the 1940s and 1950s. It's also true that the GI bill—which guaranteed lower mortgages and paid college tuition stipends for WWII veterans like our fictional heroes John Young and his cousin Joe—also gave an important leg up in America in this regard (except for black American GIs, whom the US government excluded,[23] thereby contributing to generations of dramatic economic racial disparity).

Unions did increase real wages for a whole class of workers, enabling more Americans to buy cars and a home in the suburbs. However, many would also argue that organized labor became a victim of its own success and inability to flex over the years. Today, for example, private sector union membership is at an all-time low, despite so many historic wins.

(So *are* unions still useful and relevant for workers in today's economy? Stay tuned. We'll examine that topic soon in the pages to come.)

Women Join the Workforce

By 1940, America's economy was on the way to recovery as it began to assist in the war overseas by manufacturing defense products. From tanks and ammunition to uniforms and electronics, America's factories began to crank up production.

And then, just as the newly robust economy was finally putting an end to hardship experienced during the Great Depression, the Japanese bombed Pearl Harbor. Suddenly, a country that had been divided about entering a foreign war for the second time in a quarter century galvanized into action and officially joined the war.

But because American men were sent overseas to fight, America's factories faced serious worker shortages. And that's when American women came to the rescue. They worked in construction, drove trucks, cut lumber, and, most notably, staffed the country's factories building trains, planes, and ships for the war effort. Rosie the Riveter was a cultural icon, embodying the can-do spirit of women in the workforce who picked up where men had left off.

More than 40,000 women also enlisted, serving as logistical support for soldiers as well as nurses on the front lines, even piloting stateside missions to ferry planes from one place to another.[24] In 1948, women were finally officially recognized as part of the armed services with the passage of the Women's Armed Services Integration Act.[25]

Women never really left the workforce after that. What was once men's work became women's work, too. As America's economy expanded into high gear during the 20 years after the war, women went to college, traded their aprons for corner offices, and attempted to share in the rewards of a healthy economy.[26]

Women moving into the workforce was a major disruptive event in society and when they remained after the war, it forever changed the face of America's workforce. For the first time in history, women were more likely to remain single, marry later, get an advanced degree, and postpone childbirth. With the advent of childcare—and the legalization of birth control pills in 1960—they spent more years in the labor force and stayed at jobs longer.

And, with less social stigma around divorce, more women were relying on their own salaries (instead of a spouse's), which increased their participation in the labor force even more. In 1950, just 34% of the workforce was made up of women. But by 2000, that number had climbed to 60%.[27]

As the demand for labor increased, women settled in to working outside the home, staking their claim to a piece of the economic pie. They championed the civil rights movement, the women's rights movement, and legislation promoting equal employment opportunity in the 1960s.

Segregation Gives Way to Integration

It may surprise you to learn that one of the very first organizations to embrace integration was actually the United States military. Every ethnicity was subject to the draft. The 16 million Americans who served in the World War included one million African Americans, along with plenty of Japanese Americans, Chinese Americans, and Native Americans. (It should be noted, however, that they still served in segregated units even though the US military was an equal opportunity drafter. It wasn't until 1948 that true integration was achieved after President Truman abolished military discrimination with an executive order.)

After the war, Major League Baseball was also at the forefront of organizations embracing change. In 1947, Jackie Robinson broke the color barrier in professional baseball when he signed with the Brooklyn Dodgers, officially signaling the end of segregation in baseball and the end of the Negro Leagues that had operated in America for nearly 70 years.[28] Arguably, it was not until the advent of the civil rights movement, however, that real, albeit slow, gains would be made by black Americans in the workplace.

And, during the postwar era, America was still very much a segregated society. Apartheid still existed . . . both blatantly in the Jim Crow American South or by the de facto segregation in the North. However, thanks to seminal Supreme Court cases in the 1950s, this finally began to shift.

Cases such as *Brown vs. Board of Education*[29] improved access to education for minorities. A growing movement among African Americans for social and economic justice culminated in a series of hard-fought—often with blood—legislative victories such as the Voting Rights Act and the Civil Rights Act of 1964.

Also known as Title VII, that important piece of legislation at last wedged open the door for minorities and other "protected classes" to finally earn a more equal slice of the American economic pie. (Despite these gains, of course, America still grapples with the devastating effects of structural racism all these years later. There are still far too many ways in which the criminal justice system and lack of educational and training opportunities contribute to huge economic and health disparities for black Americans today. Passionate, widespread protests across the US in the summer and fall of 2020 underline that reality.)

With such huge disruptive forces reconfiguring the American workplace in the 1960s, it was hard to imagine that yet another seismic disruption was about to occur . . . one that would upend the world of work in simply unimaginable new ways.

And that was the rise of technology.

Sorting the Winners from the Losers

In the early 1970s, the floppy disk and ethernet were invented. By the time Steve Jobs and Steve Wozniak rigged up their first Apple computer near the end of that decade, word processing was also fast becoming a reality.

And, as computers became more widespread, large corporations came of age, too. Univac, which designed the first American computer for business in the 1950s, was soon replaced by big names like the Digital Equipment Corporation (DEC), which designed the first minicomputer.

This new technological influence would also begin to sort the winners from the losers in business. Those companies that could adapt to the ever-shifting business landscape thrived and those that didn't see change coming faded into obscurity relatively quickly.

The Eastman Kodak Company, for example, famously failed when it neglected to transition to digital photography when the trend picked up steam. After more than 100 years dominating the photographic film industry, it froze in the face of change, eventually filing for Chapter 11 bankruptcy in 2012. The kicker? Kodak developed the first digital camera *in its very own lab*.[30]

Sometimes companies learned the hard way that if they tried to introduce a disruptive technology through their existing business, they'd fail. Internal politics and business processes would essentially sabotage the new model from taking hold.

DEC, for instance, was so focused on selling computers to enterprises that it missed its moment to flex by selling personal computers. Hewlett Packard was so focused on its profitable laser printer division—which sold laser printers to companies—that its sales force pushed back when it tried to introduce an inexpensive ink jet printer for consumers.

The ink jet printer was based on a different model: a low price point for the printer itself with profit in the reusable cartridges consumers would purchase. It was a classic disruptive technology. But HP couldn't get its reps to sell the product. The ink jet languished in the warehouse.

The Hewlett Packard experience points to an important differentiator between companies that often transcend changing markets and those that do not. As Professor Cocron explains it, "Mediocre companies frequently perceive new products as cannibalizing profitable existing product lines, while great companies do not."

Eventually, Hewlett Packard recognized that sales representatives who were successful at selling laser printers to large enterprises were never going to be motivated to sell inkjet printers to consumers. Generating urgency during a changing market and shift from laser printers to ink jets was a tough sell to a manager.

Rational managers just couldn't get on board with the idea of spending time selling a new product in which the company had made a substantial investment in hopes of future sales instead of the product that was already generating plenty of profit with existing customers. It just didn't fly with them.

HP learned that talking to sales representatives for laser printers was probably the worst way to assess the viability of a new consumer market for a less expensive ink jet printer. Sales reps were sure that consumers wouldn't be interested. (Actually, HP's lack of vision wasn't so different from Henry Ford's experience considering the market for his first Model T he famously said, "If I asked customers what they wanted, they would have said they wanted a faster horse.")

HP finally tackled this internal cultural obstacle by creating a new ink jet–only sales force with entrepreneurial spirit in a smaller and more intimate all-new division. The company then isolated the new division far from its headquarters in a remote location. Separate accounting and administrative functions for the fledgling division created even more of a cocoon for the new business to germinate in. And that is when ink jet printer sales finally gained traction.

The Tech Boom Accelerates

We have moved from a period when information was scare to one in which information is abundant. After the invention of radio near end of the 19th century, it took more than 30 years until the invention of the television and widespread use of the telephone.

Even though the television was invented in 1927, it wasn't found in most American homes until the mid-1950s. It would be another 10 years before some homes even had a color set. And 10 years more before those televisions were entertaining children with video games such as Pong, the popular table tennis game where you could control your TV screen through the use of the Magnavox Odyssey, the very first console video gaming system.

But fast forward to the 1980s, 1990s, and the beginning of the 21st century, and the pace of technological innovation starts to significantly speed up. The 1980s saw the home video game market heat up with the release of Atari and Sega Genesis, followed by PlayStation and Nintendo 64 in the 1990s . . . eventually giving way to the Xbox360 and Wii. Incredibly, the fax machine—a retro technology first developed in the 1950s—also enjoyed widespread use during the very same period.

Meanwhile, the internet, which had been the purview of researchers and Silicon Valley nerds for several decades, morphed into the World Wide Web and found its way into many American households by 2001.

Cell phones, first concepted in the early 1970s, were introduced by Motorola in the early 1980s at a $4,000 price point.[31] But with a major price drop by the late 1990s, America followed Europe's lead and adopted them in mass. Everyone owned a cell phone by then, abruptly putting the pager industry out of business and making the conditions ripe to embrace yet another disruptive invention: Steve Jobs's iPhone in 2007.

In one tech round-up, 4,000 UK consumers voted the iPhone one of the greatest inventions of all time, beating out the toilet and the wheel![32] Perhaps that's because our phones seem so indispensable to daily life today. Thanks to the ever-expanding world of apps, the touchscreen technology connects us with friends, families, and colleagues, as well as takeout options for dinner. We monitor our daily steps, quality of sleep, and likes on social media.

What is most striking looking back at the history of the tech boom is the pace of change in the last 100 years. Innovation is arriving faster and faster than it ever has before.

Dictation, for example, has moved to transcription from tape recordings to voice recognition software. BlackBerries were quickly and completely replaced by smartphones. Slide presentations moved to PowerPoint to webinars. Relocation and office expenses for off-site workers have been abandoned in favor of telecommuting.[33]

In large part, it's the rapid advance of technology that enabled us to flex so quickly and successfully in spring 2020 during the COVID-19 pandemic. The lightning-fast transmission of information is reshaping industries and reputations in breathtaking speed, creating feelings of being overwhelmed and unimaginable new opportunities in the world of work.

So what does it all mean? You can call it *change*. Or you can call it *disruption*. You can call it whatever you like, but recognize it as *progress*.

Progress Is Not a Dirty Word

Progress refers to advances in technology, science, and social organization . . . ultimately to improve the human condition. In fact, President Theodore Roosevelt (a Republican originally and later a member of the Progressive Party) felt that "wise progressivism and wise conservatism go hand in hand."[34]

Unfortunately, in some circles today, the term *progressive* is equated with a liberal political view. But that's just not true. *Progressive* is an adjective that denotes, quite simply, progress. Specifically, Merriam Webster defines it as "of, relating to, or characterized by progress" and "making use of or interested in new ideas, findings, or opportunities."[35]

There has always been progress and change. The difference is that now it's coming much, much faster, particularly with respect to how it affects the world of work. Today, we are seeing a shift from the evolution of work from a rigid hierarchy and fixed work hours to a flatter structure with flexible work hours.

With the onset of the COVID-19 pandemic, employer resistance to working from home suddenly evaporated. Instead of a perk enjoyed by lucky freelancers and leagues of Silicon Valley 20-something coders, working from home went mainstream as most of America took meetings on Zoom and employers began to wonder if they really needed that 4,000 square feet of office space after all.

Instead of people in power hoarding proprietary on-site data and information, cloud technology and online forums facilitate collaboration and sharing. Just a few years ago, email was a primary form of communication. Today, it's quickly taking a back seat to texting.

Siloed, fragmented companies are becoming connected and engaged. Employees are no longer content to climb the corporate ladder. Rather, they want to build their *own* ladder . . . the one that suits their personal vision of what success looks like for *them*.

Perhaps most important, smart leaders are beginning to relax their grip on control to "follow from the front."[36] Those who bring in the most money, or are the best at navigating internal politics, are on the way out.

Who will the winners be? Those who stand in service of the people who work for them, busting barriers and removing obstacles so they can do their jobs effectively.

This then is what *progress* looks like in the world of work.

Key Learning Points

1. Disruption is inevitable. Huge shifts in how business works has always reshaped the world of work. The difference today is that those seismic shifts are coming faster and faster. Savvy businesses understand they must disrupt or *be* disrupted.

(continued)

2. Companies exist because they can absorb the transaction costs of doing business more efficiently than an individual can. This value proposition still holds true today. When individuals can do it better and more cheaply, they can—and will—disrupt an industry rapidly. (Stay tuned for more on the gig economy.)

3. The organized labor movement has delivered important gains for American workers, including collective bargaining, standardized hours, a minimum wage, and enforceable legal protections for worker safety.

4. Major disruptive events throughout American economic history—such as women in the workforce, integration, and the rise of technology—have set the foundation for the kinds of changes reshaping the world of work today.

5. *Progress* is not a dirty word! Although the word is often conflated with liberal political values, it really just characterizes the use of new ideas, findings, and opportunities.

3 The People Who Work Are Changing

If you change the way you look at things, the things you look at change.

Source: Wayne W. Dyer, Change Your Thoughts, Change Your Life,
Hay House, Inc., © 2007.

Not long ago, I supervised two young associates who were enigmas to me, Tom and Jenny. Looking back, I can recognize that my experience with the two of them echoed that of leaders in organizations all over the country. But at the time, I did not think beyond my own situation.

It all started when I asked the two of them to meet a tight client deadline that would require several late evenings at the office. This is not an unusual request at a law firm, particularly when the request is made on behalf of an important client relationship that's been nurtured for years. Associates are simply expected to work the hours it takes to complete a task assigned by a senior partner in the firm.

At least that's how it worked when I came up in the legal profession. If someone more senior made a request of me, I got it done. *On time. No questions asked.* Whether I had to stay up all night or spend all weekend at the office. Everyone understood that that was just how it worked. It's what we signed up for when we chose to enter the profession. And it was the only way to eventually be rewarded as a partner.

So imagine my shock and frustration when Tom looked at me after just such a request and said, "I'm sorry but I have other evening commitments this week, so I'll be needing to leave at 5 pm."

Or, possibly even more shocking, when Jenny told me, "I didn't have a good experience with this client so I'd prefer not to work on this project." When I looked a bit aghast, Tom assured me that he'd "be available by phone" if I needed him and Jenny said she'd be happy to help out with any other client. Then Tom added, "I'll definitely be checking my phone after my workout. I can jump online and address anything you need. I'm even happy to FaceTime if you'd like."

What?

If you've ever had a version of an experience like this with a more junior employee, then you may be chuckling a bit at my reaction. If you haven't, I can assure you one is coming.

The way millennials work and what they value is radically different than their older colleagues, which is leading to a lot of generational friction in workplaces across the country today. Millennials are on the rise in a big way.

And that's not all that's reshaping our labor force. The face of America's workforce is changing. Marginalized LGBTQ (lesbian/gay/bisexual/trans/queer) workers are asserting their right to being recognized in the workplace as the equals they are. Additionally, people with disabilities have made great progress toward equal access to the workplace.

Women—who have been in the workforce for more than 70 years now—are redoubling their efforts to end discrimination and sexual harassment. They won't put up with it anymore. And neither should you in your organization.

Let's take a deeper dive to consider some of these radical demographic changes that are reshaping the world of work.

Crunching the Numbers

Here's how the labor force broke down in 2010 (the most recent census year): there were 38 million baby boomers (birthdates 1946 to 1964); 57 million millennials (birthdates 1981 to 1996), who are also known as Gen Y; and 53 million Gen Xers (birthdates 1965 to 1980).[1]

Plus, don't forget about Gen Z, born between 1997 and 2014. There are 65 million Gen Zers today, and they account for about 40% of American consumers in 2020.[2]

It's pretty clear that the youngsters far outnumber the oldsters in the American workforce today. But what is "old" exactly?

Well, it depends whom you're asking. In one survey, 51% of respondents said you're old once you're in your 70s. But then, when responses are considered by the age of the respondent, that notion changes. As you might anticipate, Gen Xers said people are old in their 40s, and baby boomers and their even older colleagues pegged old at age 80.[3]

Also, the 2017 United States Census Bureau predicted that in 2030, for the first time in history, there will be more folks ready for retirement (age 65) than there are children (under age 18).[4] Essentially, one out of every five residents will be retirement age. And that decade will usher in a new era of slower population growth, when immigrants make up net growth in the workforce to offset the deaths of baby boomers.

Don't underestimate the impact of these monumental changes. In the coming years, baby boomers will hang on tenaciously to their place in the workforce. After all, over the course of the 20th century, the human lifespan has improved from an average of 49 to 79 years.[5] And it won't be unusual for children born today to live to 100. So people are participating in the world of work much longer than ever before.

Many are a lot less interested in retiring at age 65 than their parents were. Some are working into their golden years because they need the income. Others want to work to keep their brains sharp and their bodies strong. Many men and women today—ages 40, 50, and 60 years old—are even starting new businesses as a lifetime of financial savings funds newfound creative freedom.

Still others want to continue to work to avoid the social isolation that came for their parents in old age. They're passing up their parents' retirement fantasies of playing canasta and golf in favor of remaining engaged at work. They're no longer motivated by promotions or fancy job titles; rather, they want to share a lifetime of acquired skills and experience by mentoring the next generation or finding other ways to give back late in life.

So although the future of the American workplace is definitely millennial (and Gen Z), it's also important to remember that baby boomers won't be leaving any time soon. That's one of the reasons it's so critical for employers to stamp out ageism in the workplace. When a recruiter places an ad looking for someone to join a "young, dynamic team" or laughs about a "senior moment," that's ageism at work (even though younger employees might not recognize it).

And that's never okay. Companies looking to recruit older workers need to avoid using words that exclude them. Instead of *savvy, young,* or *energetic,* try words like *motivated, dedicated,* or *driven* instead. Be sure that marketing materials for recruitment reflect the diversity your organization is seeking. (Do photos depict older people as well as younger people? People of color? Nonbinary-gender non-conforming people? Women?)

Along the same lines, be aware of the ways in which you're reaching out to older employment prospects through your recruitment efforts. Are you only advertising online or at the local universities? Consider reaching out through newspapers, too. Remember to promote benefits such as gym memberships, flexible work arrangements, and education on topics such as retirement planning.

Employers Need to Flex

The demographic shifts taking place today will require a whole lot more from employers who want to be competitive in the years ahead. They will need to ramp up ways to meet the needs of boomers even as they redesign the workplace to accommodate the preferences of millennials (Gen Y), Gen X, and eventually, Gen Z.

On the one hand, companies recognize that boomers still hold the lion's share of wealth in this country. And even though the oldest millennials turned 40 in 2020—making them the largest adult generation and also the best educated generation—they hold just 3% of the wealth in America today.[6] This "longevity economy" will drive the economy in the foreseeable future. So imagine the possibilities if organizations would actively recruit older Americans who understand their aging customer base to then develop well-calibrated products and services to meet their changing needs. Forward-thinking organizations are tapping the wealth of experience, insight, and wisdom in older employees that younger employees just can't match.

That's leading to some creative strategies by America's companies. For example, CVS offers a "Snowbird" program that allows older workers—pharmacists, photo supervisors, and cosmetic consultants—to transfer locations seasonally. (IBM has a similar program.) The National Institutes of Health actively recruits smart people over age 50 at job fairs and then lures them with flex schedules, telecommuting opportunities, and exercise classes. Even Home Depot hires retired construction workers to advise customers on its sales floor.[7]

Another recruitment strategy on the rise is "returnships"—essentially *internships*—in which retired adults with a gap in work experience are onboarded and trained during a trial period and then hired if all goes well. It's essentially a career reboot for experienced workers.

The concept is also putting stay-at-home moms, younger workers caring for older parents, and others with gaps in their résumé back to work very effectively. And the idea is getting traction in a wide range of industries, from tech companies and health care to banking and non-profits.[8]

But even as companies work to hang on to boomer employees, they will also need to step up their ability to understand and respond to the aspirations of their increasingly younger employees.

Remember Jenny and Tom? The pair of millennials who wanted to FaceTime me from the gym instead of staying late to complete my project? It turns out they are not so unusual in their approach to the world of work when it comes to others of their generation (and beyond).

What's most important to millennials is radically different than it was for prior generations. If we don't change to accommodate the needs and communication styles younger generations prefer, we risk seeming tone-deaf to the workforce of tomorrow.

They may be struggling with disconnect and cynicism in some ways, but they are also sociable, self-confident, street smart, and value extreme fun. Most important, they value personal attention.

Initially, I had literally no idea what to say to Jenny and Tom when my request was so roundly rebuffed. But then I thought about some sage words a valued partner once offered me. She said that *everyone* has baggage. She told me that the key to successful communication is knowing what's in your suitcase *and* the other person's.

So the three of us sat down together for a chat to unpack these attitudes. I pointed out that neither of them were likely to make partner at the firm if they continued to respond in the same way.

To my surprise, Tom said becoming a partner was not his goal. "Honestly, I don't want to move up," he explained to me. "I just want to make enough money as an associate to pay my bills and spend time pursuing other interests. That's what would make me happy. My wife makes a very good living and our personal time is really important to me."

When we talked further, Tom explained that his hour commute was a real time suck and he really preferred more flexible hours to skip the rush hour traffic. In fact, working remotely would really be the best option for him.

I tried to explain that "work–life balance" isn't really possible in our business. We're labor lawyers. We need to be there for our clients at a moment's notice. There are labor strikes and emergency last-minute court appearances to be managed.

Clients don't have the luxury of preplanning when a union campaign is imminent or a workplace injury occurs. So it's critical that we are available to respond *any hour of the day or night*.

But Tom and Jenny saw it differently. To them, it's not about work–life balance but rather work–life *integration*. Jenny said that to her, work–life integration means she can work from anywhere, not necessarily at the office. That she can be available by phone, FaceTime, or on the internet. When pressed, she explained that although she loves the law, it is ultimately just one of the things she is interested in devoting time to in the coming years.

She wants to simultaneously pursue other business ventures while working toward her master's degree and taking sabbatical breaks to recharge in far-flung places. Tom wants to design a future that will eventually enable him to stay home with kids as a more involved dad (while also working part-time).

There are Gen Z developers working at major Silicon Valley corporations who recoil at the idea of getting to the office before noon for a meeting but are often awake into the wee hours designing a new app. The employer who labels these workers as "unmotivated" or "lazy" risks missing out on some of the best and brightest talent in America's workforce today. Jenny and Tom are extremely talented and certainly valuable to my firm.

Retooling for the Next-Gen Workforce

It took me a bit but eventually I recognized that Jenny and Tom might be on to something. After all, they've watched the career arc of their parents and it sometimes seemed like a lot to give for so-called job satisfaction and fulfillment. Many millennials are just plain refusing to accept the idea that they must spend every waking minute toiling away at a job to achieve some dated and undefined notion of "success."

And who's to say they are wrong? In my industry, for example, burnout takes an incredible toll on attorneys who often feel like they're on call 24 hours a day with no way to disconnect. In one survey, more than 30% of 3,800 attorneys surveyed said they felt depressed and another 60% reported feeling anxious.[9] That is no way to live.

In industries experiencing epidemic rates of stress-related illness like these, it's critical for employers to inquire after employees' health, provide time off for wellness, and acknowledge these challenges rather than looking the other way. Nothing substitutes for a culture where it's okay to ask for help. Wellness programs and assistance programs can make all the difference.

So I say, good for those coming up in the world of work who say yes to alternatives that preserve their mental health. Some 20-, 30-, and 40-somethings are even going a step further. Inspired by the FIRE (financial independence retire early) movement, they are living frugally—forgoing Starbucks lattes and the latest iPhone—in a push to leave the rat race much, much sooner than their parents ever did.

They're stashing six-figure incomes in retirement accounts instead. And this isn't some fringe movement. Today, FIRE has more than 700,000 members on a financial independence subreddit (a topic-focused subcategory on the popular news aggregator Reddit). One FIRE-related blog boasts more than 30 million unique viewers since 2011.[10]

Millennials such as Jenny and Tom are also "disrupters" in the very best sense of the word. In other words, they are reshaping the way we work, often through their use of the latest technology. Although it may seem to many of us as disruptive, as we have seen, disruption has always been the hallmark of progress. To be a disruptor is to move forward in business, to create ripples and eventually waves in a virtuous cycle of success.

Today, at my law firm and thousands across the country, it's possible for lawyers to work part-time and still be on track to succeed. Smart employers flex to design benefits and career tracks that meet the needs of a changing workforce.

At my firm, for example, we sponsor and participate in community diversity initiatives and offer a new attorney survival skills program to smooth the onboarding process for new recruits. A firm-wide mentoring system pairs each associate with a partner-mentor as well.

We also provide up to 12 weeks of paid parental leave to employees who are primary caregivers after a birth, adoption, or foster care placement and four weeks of paid leave to secondary caregivers. Remember, millennials view "bring your child to work" days as an outmoded concept. Instead, they flock to employers with onsite "bring your baby to work *every day*" programs.

But aren't infant-at-work policies a distraction? Actually, it's just the opposite. It's easy for parents to soothe babies onsite. As long as an employer's expectations are clear and provide for some flexibility, these programs routinely improve employee retention, reduce health care costs, enable earlier return-to-work dates for parents, and improve the perception of the organization as a family-friendly business.[11] It's a win for parents, babies, and employers.

The four-day work week is another way to help millennials achieve more of that work–life integration they crave (and thereby reduce turnover). A recent Gallup report estimated millennial turnover costs the US economy $30.5 billion annually.[12] In 2019, Adams County School District in Colorado became the first school district in a major metro area to move to a four-day work week. The goal? To attract and retain more talent.

So far, it's worked, with more applicants and lower turnover in the pilot year of the program. Perpetual Guardian, a New Zealand–based financial services company, analyzed results of its switch to a four-day, 30-hour work week and found that employees performed the same amount of work but reported significant improvement in work–life balance.

Another tactic gaining steam is "conversational recruiting." It's a high-tech-high-touch talent acquisition strategy that keeps employers in close contact with job candidates every step of the way. Remember, millennials are frustrated by slow, cumbersome hiring processes that leave them hanging. Those tools and processes feel out of step with the instant gratification of social media and technology that has always been a part of their lives.

Instead, use a Chatbot through a texting or messaging app to expedite the application process and keep candidates posted on status of filling the position. Meet millennials and Gen Zers where they live: on FaceTime, Google Hangouts, Zoom, and Skype. They're great ways for both employers and candidates to gauge an initial impression before investing more time and energy into on-site interviews.

Likewise, when hiring managers text applicants to keep them posted on the status of their job application, applicants remain more engaged. One study showed such texts had a 98% open rate![13] Overall, it's an easy way to collect information, make appointments, and ask legitimate, routine business questions.

Companies already using such tools are early adopters of technological innovation. They seek out new ways to make the workplace inclusive, diverse, and accessible. Conversely, leaders who roll their eyes at applicants they deem to be "snowflakes" will lose out, succumbing to disruption as so many companies have throughout history.

Coming up fast behind millennials such as Jenny and Tom is Gen Z, the newest generation of workers. Older Gen Zers are new to the workforce, about 24 years old today. And although they are a few years away from leaving their mark, make no mistake: they, too, will reshape the workforce in the years to come.

It might surprise you, for example, to learn that Gen Z, "the digital generation," actually prefers face-to-face work interactions. They see themselves as the hardest-working generation of workers, but they also don't like feeling "forced to work." They want a say over their schedule and aren't interested in working back-to-back shifts.

In a slight twist on millennials' experience watching their parents work too much, Gen Z grew up while their parents lost homes and jobs in the 2008 global recession. In fact, many went to work early to help make ends meet or pay for their own expenses as teenagers.[14]

Gen Z is anxious. They don't feel confident they can meet employers' expectations in negotiating, networking, working long hours, speaking confidently in front of crowds, resolving conflicts, or being managed by another person. Fully 34% of study participants said their anxiety is holding them back from success at work![15] Employers who flex will understand how to successfully manage the tension that might occur between this group and the larger population of millennials in their workplace. This will be no small feat.

The Value of Mentor Programs

Imagine for a moment what a company could accomplish if it paired the judgment and wisdom of older workers with the creative talent and enthusiasm of younger employees who need more confidence and experience. What if relationships could be nurtured so that both individuals received mentoring on targeted skills they were seeking to improve?

But wait, you may be saying. That's a recipe for conflict. Generations don't always get along so great.

And that's fair. There has always been intergenerational conflict. Just think back to the 1960s counterculture as young hippies "turned on, tuned in, and dropped out," much to the chagrin of their parents, members of the Greatest Generation, whose core values included personal responsibility, commitment, and a serious work ethic. We called that "the generation gap."

We're seeing it today, too, with trending of the catchphrase "Okay, Boomer," Gen Z's rallying cry that baby boomers and even millennials just don't "get it" when it comes to everything from attitudes about dyed hair to the urgency of climate change.

But just as there has always been intergenerational conflict, so too has there always been value in intergenerational *connection*. It's the natural order of things, even. Around the world, just as busy young parents have long traded babysitting by grandparents for elder care, so too can we extend intergenerational reciprocity for the good of the business. Now is the time for the world of work to capitalize on such opportunities.

That Gen Zer who struggles with the basics of navigating work relationships? She could sit in on meetings and presentations with that 70-year-old retired executive who just enrolled in the organization's returnship program.

Then she could explain to that executive why and how to Tweet, use an Instagram account for marketing, or offer lessons on navigating that state-of-the-art software that human resources just installed on his computer that he may have been resistant to use. Just as moody teenagers with too much time on their hands and poor grades are paired with retirees who could use a Facebook tutor through creative mentor programs at local nursing homes, work mentorship programs are full of promise in America today.

The Rise of the #MeToo Movement

Just as generational differences are reshaping the work landscape, so too are women doubling down on their fight for equality. Despite their steadfast participation in the American workplace since World War II, the leadership at many organizations still remains overwhelmingly male. And this is a tragedy for a number of reasons.

First, such organizations perpetuate outdated stereotypes and kindle a toxic culture that demeans women. When the #MeToo hashtag went viral on Twitter in 2017, thousands of women around the world broke decades of silence in shared solidarity about their personal experiences of sexual harassment and assault in the workplace.

For the first time, women refused to stay silent en masse, pointing out the inappropriate behaviors of male supervisors and colleagues throughout their careers, holding men accountable in positions of power from Hollywood to Wall Street.

The national dialogue that followed boosted the visibility of women passed over for promotion in favor of less-qualified male coworkers due to sexual favors refused or simply for being too direct, assertive, or demanding . . . all leadership characteristics rewarded in men. #MeToo breathed new life into the women's rights movement that began back in the 1960s.

There's still a long way to go in the pursuit of equal opportunity for women, but thanks to #MeToo, there is a renewed push for gender parity in corporate America today. In 2019, Bloomberg launched a gender equality index that tracks the progress of 230 companies committed to advancing women in the workplace. Between 2014 and 2017, they report a 40% increase in female executive positions as investors have pushed back against boards that are not diverse enough.[16]

The reality is that the world of work was originally set up by men for men. When men moved from their farms into factories during the Industrial Revolution, there was no thought to what women might need. And although that may have made sense back when workers were predominately male, that entire dated system—still in place despite the fact that women make up 47% of the workforce today[17]—has become discriminatory.

Not only that, but for the first time, in 2019, women made up the majority of the college-educated workforce.[18] Women have also outnumbered men in law school classrooms for several years in a row now.[19] And the reality is that the 66 million working women today are expected to grow to 92 million by 2050. It's critical that there is wage parity for women moving forward.

And yet, women still bear the majority of responsibility for childcare and housework in their families, even if they work full-time. During the recent COVID-19 pandemic, one in three essential workers were women, risking their lives on the front lines of America's race to stop the infection. Although the number of male nurses has tripled since the 1970s, 9 out of 10 nurses are still female.[20] Nonwhite women were even more likely to be essential workers during the pandemic.

However, if equality for women is a non-negotiable goal in the American workplace, we must also empower men to share the disproportionate burden of childcare women shoulder. Until work culture recognizes and responds to the need for men to take leave for parenting responsibilities as women do, women will be doing most of the heavy lifting here. In too many workplaces in America, men who ask for leave to parent new babies are still stigmatized and risk derailing a career with such a request.

This may well change as millennials continue to rise. They are likely to create increasing pressure on employers in this regard. They just won't stand for ridiculous human resources policies that don't match their reality. They're looking for companies with flextime and other policies that accommodate the parenting challenges they face without financial and career penalties.

You know who else the world of work was originally set up for? White people. Not only are there a dearth of women in the boardroom, but black Americans and other people of color are also not well represented. Whether through unconscious or overt bias over decades, parity has been impossible to achieve here so far.

In the very eye of the storm during the COVID-19 pandemic in summer and fall 2020, America also wrestled anew with the uncomfortable truth of its institutional racist past during widespread protests. This tragic history has contributed to wide economic disparities today between white Americans and black Americans. The data shows that black Americans can expect to earn up to $1 million less over their life-times than white Americans.[21]

In his excellent article "Are You Willing to Give Up Your Priv-ilege?"[22] Daren Walker, president of the Ford Foundation, calls on business leaders to actively unwind the many unfairly structured incentives distorting our economy and for American businesses to surrender special privileges and benefits. These include everything from legacy college admissions and tax policies that bolster existing wealth, to corporate dogma that puts shareholder value above that of other stakeholders. These are worthy ideas.

Isn't it time we redesign our country to work for *everyone*?

Diversity and Inclusion Start at the Top

When it comes to hardwiring a culture of inclusion and diversity, it flows from the board and senior executives down to rank-and-file workers. That's just one reason why it's so critical to include women and people of color in the C suite. Organizations with diverse senior executives also benefit through more varied skill sets and less discrim-ination, which filters through the organization's efforts to recruit, promote, and retain more talent.

And yet, consider existing gender disparities. Despite the fact that nearly 40% of managers and 40% of MBA graduates are women,[23] they are *still* largely absent from the C suite and the boardroom. Although controversial, some organizations have looked to hiring quotas as a way to close such gaps.

In fact, California is the first state in the union to require publicly held companies to have at least one female on their board of directors by the end of 2019, with two required on boards of five, and three on boards of six or more by the end of 2021.[24] Although it's too early to understand the long-term impact of legislating diversity, it's likely to create the kind of critical mass of women that makes a difference in boardroom dynamics.

There is economic urgency for leadership diversity, too. In fact, one study demonstrated that companies with at least three women on their board outperform competitors by 1.2% through better productivity and more diverse ideas.[25] Maybe that's one reason why nearly one-third of global S&P 500 companies include three or more women on their boards.[26]

When firms moved from having no women in corporate leadership positions to a 30% share of female leadership, they earned a 1% increase in net margin. And that translated to a 15% increase in profitability. In my experience working with many companies, decisions that favor diversity and inclusiveness are nearly always rewarded by the market. It's just good business.

Harvard Business Review conducted a study of 22,000 global firms on just this topic. When it examined what it determined to be "profitable" firms—those with a net margin of 6.4%—the financial effect of more diverse and inclusive leadership was very clear.[27]

Still, in another study[28] of 200 companies with $100 million or more in funding, two years after #MeToo went viral on Twitter and around the globe, 60% of organizations still do not have a single female board member. That same study found that women held just 7% of board seats and that less than 10% of boards included more than one woman.

So are quotas *really* the answer? Affirmative action and quotas are not the same thing. Indeed in 1978, the US Supreme Court declared affirmative action constitutional while it invalidated the use of strict racial quotas in higher education.[29] This and later cases found that although "race-conscious" factors were acceptable as just one criterion in the admissions process in order to achieve the benefits of a diverse student body, strict quotas that used it as the sole factor violated the proscriptions against discrimination based on race found in the Civil Rights Act of 1964.[30]

Well-designed affirmative action programs seek to eliminate discrimination for *all* marginalized people. As Lyndon D. Johnson explained[31] in a 1965 commencement address at Howard University, "We seek not just legal equity but human ability, not just equality as a right and a theory but equality as a fact and equality as a result."

Unlike quotas, quality affirmative action programs don't set a pre-determined, inflexible result. Rather, they strive to increase diversity through a sophisticated mix of targeted recruitment, employee support, and development programs. That's a far better approach—rather than quotas—to recruiting the best and brightest talent while also filling gaps in diversity.

When companies recognize they're missing out on critical voices and ideas of women, African Americans, Hispanics, disabled employees, or LGBTQ individuals because they aren't well represented in the workforce, it can broaden the scope of recruiting. For instance, in our previous discussion of how to recruit more boomers, I advised running newspaper ads—electronic and print—instead of just recruiting at the local university. You have to go where your prospects are.

The same holds true when it comes to increasing diversity for other segments of the population. You're looking for more African Americans for your law firm? You should be actively recruiting at historically black colleges like Howard University in Washington, DC, and the National Bar Association, the nation's oldest and largest national network of predominantly African American attorneys and judges.

You'd like to hire more LGBTQ individuals? Recruit at the National LGBT Bar Association's Lavender Law Conference & Career

Fair for attorneys as my firm does or the Out & Equal Workplace Summit. Ask for advice from your local LGBT center. Looking to add more employees with disabilities? Check out the Sierra Group in Philadelphia, a disability recruiter that runs a job posting board and conducts training.

Sometimes, despite our most creative recruiting efforts, it can be difficult to recruit the talent we're looking for. Institutional disadvantages—usually invisible to people of privilege—are baked into American society that limit the kind of professional upward mobility that shapes the kind of top talent we're seeking.

When motivated, talented individuals are passed over for educational and career opportunities or promotion due to discrimination—or even through unconscious bias, or they can't qualify due to systematic biases, or they lack access to critical training—we all lose out on their gifts and skills. Those individuals are out there looking for work but are sorely lacking in institutional opportunities.

That's why your organizations have an obligation to change that. Those of us with privilege also have a great responsibility. Can't find qualified female executives? Start, or join a women-in-leadership training course at your local chamber of commerce.

Every industry has its own industry networking groups—many are organized by interest groups, such as women in engineering, for example—so that's a great place to find individuals looking to qualify for training and opportunities. Be sure to join and become active in organizations within your industry that focus on promoting diversity and inclusion.

Local colleges and universities also frequently host job fairs and internships to promote both broad and narrow types of diversity, so reach out to individuals there, too. Does your organization offer a diversity internship program? It's a great way to heighten the profile of your company and elevate its standing in the eyes of employees.

Anything you can do to broadcast your support of a community will draw that community to you. Participate in Pride events, create employee networking groups, and participate in surveys, such as Bloomberg's gender equality index survey or the Human Rights Campaign's annual corporate equality index survey. By hiring more minorities, you'll be promoting them, too, actively championing change.

America's Future Is Not White

Why is there so much anti-immigrant sentiment in American politics today when it comes to nonwhite people? Many white Americans feel threatened by the increasing number of people of color who live in the US. In fact, whites will officially become a minority—making up just 49.5% of the population—in the US by 2045.[32] In many states, for example, California, this will occur much sooner.

Hispanics or Latinx will count for 24.6%, Asians 7.9%, 3.8% will be multiracial, and .9% will be classified as "other." And, starting in 2020, less than half of American children are projected to be white.[33] (Nonwhites already make up the majority of American newborns and students in public K–12 schools.)

As a group, minorities are younger than whites overall. And that means that the minority tipping point for Gen Z and beyond will come as early as 2027. By 2060, the Census projects that white Americans will make up just 36% of the population under age 18, and Latinx will account for 32%.[34]

Already today, there is a surge of minority workers joining the American workforce. In fact, for the very first time in history,

beginning in 2019, the majority of American hires in their prime—
ages 25 to 54—were people of color.[35] The big influx is primarily
due to women of color going to work. And that's driving Latinx and
African American unemployment to historic lows.

The reason behind this? For one thing, employers are reaching out
to nontraditional candidates more frequently as they cast a wider net to
recruit top talent. For another, cultural attitudes among Latinx women
about staying home with children are shifting. Increasingly, they, too,
are joining the workforce.

In a striking contrast to the political narrative about other countries sending us "their worst," immigrants are the ones driving innovation in America today. The evidence is clear on this point: they are
more likely to attend college and earn an advanced degree as well as
to pursue careers in science, technology, engineering, and medicine.[36]
Not only a little more likely: they are more than four times as likely
than those born in America to graduate high school and twice as likely
to hold a doctorate degree![37]

One way to quantify innovation in America today would be
to consider who is acquiring patents. Care to take a guess? It's
immigrants! Although they make up just 18% of the workforce over
age 25 in the US today, they obtain 28% of high-quality patents.
(And companies where diversity is encouraged also own more of those
patents.) They're also more likely to be recognized as Nobel laureates in
physics, chemistry, medicine, and physiology.[38]

And, finally, economists widely agree that immigrants raise economic output through their contributions to the workforce. In fact,
we can thank them for contributing approximately 10% of the United
States' yearly GDP, which adds up to roughly $2 trillion![39]

Americans in favor of a market-driven, robust economy with
healthy innovation should welcome the changing face of America.

With diversity comes creative new perspectives and ideas that change the world.

The good news is that, increasingly, American companies recognize just this reality and are embracing diversity initiatives that feed these gains. And, as I said previously, organizations that report more diversity on their executive teams enjoy more innovation and better financial performance.[40]

But It's Not *Just* About Competitive Advantage

It's also about survival. (Flex or be disrupted . . . remember?)

There may have been a time when American companies felt that employing more people of color or even LGBTQ workers was an "extra" or a "nice to have." But that's frankly no longer true.

As millennials begin to dominate the workforce, they are in search of employers where the pool of workers and leaders mirrors the reality of their lives . . . their friends and families, the people they see in restaurants and in the grocery store. And that is not overwhelmingly white. Or always straight.

It's far more typical today for an average millennial or Gen Zer to have friends who are gay, trans, nonbinary, or even asexual, not to mention brown-skinned. When that millennial walks into a workplace where the management team is overwhelmingly straight, male, and white, she hears alarm bells. That company may as well hang a banner that says, "We are old and out of touch."

Millennials understand that tech teams from India and programmers from China are working with Apple and Google, both in Silicon Valley and in offices and homes around the world. Globalization has transformed the world of work in ways that extend far beyond the ability of technology to connect remote teams. Diversity is on the way to becoming the new normal.

President Donald Trump made the building of walls along the US border with Mexico a central pledge during his 2016 election campaign. And indeed, even as COVID-19 ravaged America in spring 2020, he tried to ramp up his efforts to build that wall faster. But no walls will ever halt globalization. For better or worse—whether it's the spread of a deadly virus or the ability to stop that virus with a vaccine invented by a creative multicultural team from around the world—we are all in this together.

Tomorrow's leading employers will embrace—and even celebrate—these changes or risk being left forever behind. Just as American businesses initially resisted taking employee temperatures and allowing employees to work from home during the COVID-19 pandemic—viewing such tactics as unworkable—so too will companies need to abandon outdated homogeneous American norms and look to global norms for guidance on diversity instead. The market will demand it.

What About People with Disabilities?

According to the US Census Bureau, one in five Americans will experience a disability during their lifetime. And yet, they represent the largest group of unemployed Americans.[41] Only 20% of those with disabilities are working, compared to 69% of those without disabilities. That's a devastating loss of talent.

Here's another sad reality: even progressive organizations with formalized diversity and inclusion programs are unlikely to emphasize disability in their workforce inclusion efforts. Just 7%[42] of such employers do!

Sensitivity and awareness is not enough. Rather, a robust employee accommodation protocol is required. Although barriers to full participation in the workforce depend, of course, on the disability, there is a rather large list.

They range from employers' misperceptions about hiring and accommodating someone with a disability to inaccessible workspaces and other physical barriers in the building. Many otherwise qualified individuals who are disabled also lack the assistive technology they need to access the internet or the technology training that will enable them to excel.

Companies that ignore this labor pool miss out on the very real economic benefits of employing disabled individuals. According to one study[43] of 140 organizations, those with an environment that was more inclusive of disabled employees enjoyed 28% greater revenue, a 30% higher profit margin, and *double* the net income of their less inclusive peers.

Embrace this opportunity. These prospective employees offer a rich expanded labor pool and improve your visibility as a socially responsible company. You'll also benefit from diverse perspectives and a more compassionate culture.[44]

Learn to Recognize Your Own Bias

How inclusive is your company when it comes to women, people of color, LGBTQ, and disabled employees? Have you ever done a survey to find out?

Tristan Higgins, founder of Metaclusive®, has. In fact, she's surveyed dozens of companies in her role as a consultant to help organizations become more inclusive. "You can't fix what you can't see," she explains. "Everyone is biased. In fact, the more privileged you are, the more likely you are to have blind spots." As one example, she points out that Caucasians are 80 times more likely than African Americans to feel people are caring toward each other at work.

Higgins points out that we have moved beyond the tolerance of the 1980s, the idea of diversity in the 1990s, and even the concept of inclusion that debuted in the 2000s. Today, successful workplace cultures are defined by a sense of *belonging*.

And that's why she coined the term *metaclusive*. "The term reflects a sense of belonging that transcends diversity and inclusion . . . where every person is represented, valued, and accepted. Metaclusive organizations are more profitable and just plain happier places to be," she notes.

Higgins explains that one of the most common reactions to the results of employee engagement surveys is surprise that a company has a problem at all. They may *believe* in concepts such as equal pay or offering flexibility, but when the rubber hits the road, that's just not translating to what actually occurs for every individual in the workplace. And that's a recipe for a toxic culture that compromises company performance. This is especially true for companies in which the CEO is very supportive of, but has not taken overt steps to, addressing diversity.

In a typical survey, she says that more than 60% of employees are "covering" during their day at work. In other words, they don't feel they can really claim their full identity safely. They actively downplay mannerisms, behaviors, and activities that might identify them based on race, gender, sexual orientation, religion, or disability to "fit in" and get ahead personally or professionally.

A gay man may choose not to bring his partner to a company function. Or a woman with young kids might downplay that she's a mom, working nights and weekends to demonstrate her commitment to her job instead. When it comes to LGBTQ employees, 83% feel this way. What may surprise you, though, is that 45% of *straight white male employees* are also typically covering. In such situations, employees don't have faith in management, don't feel safe at work, and aren't great at teamwork.

Becoming more aware of these unconscious biases isn't enough. That just won't fix the daily reality for black people, brown people, women, disabled individuals, or LGBTQ employees. To solve such deep-rooted issues requires policies such as "bias interruption," when rules are consistently followed to remove biases.

For example, a manager reviewing a résumé with a Caucasian-sounding name like Christopher Smith may be more likely to call that person in for an interview over the one with a name more common in African American communities. Redacted résumé reviews can right that wrong.

"The goal is to build in systems to correct biases in as many ways as you can," she adds. "Auditing the process of promotions and raises, for example, to ensure they are based on performance rather than penalizing a female employee who is maybe in the office less because she's juggling a new baby."

Because one-size-fits-all approaches and hunches don't work, it's key to diagnose specific challenges in order to target the appropriate solution. Maybe you're concerned African Americans don't feel welcome at your workplace, but you learn that they actually do . . . you've just done a poor job recruiting them. Then, instead of creating a huge celebration for Martin Luther King Day, you might, as an alternative, ramp up recruitment efforts at historically black colleges.

To effectively solve problems, it's important to assemble a team that includes representation from the group you're trying to engage. Just as able-bodied architects tend to design buildings with doors that are difficult for disabled individuals to open, so, too, can human resources head down the wrong path if, say, a white female HR rep organizes a networking group for Asian employees.

What's far more effective is an announcement that human resources is available to support and encourage (with guidance and a budget) any employee interested in starting a networking group. Then allow those employees to set appropriate priorities, with some oversight to ensure the priorities are related to the goals of the business.[45]

Learning to correct inherent biases with tools like those used by Higgins delivers big payoffs for companies looking to disrupt the competitive landscape in their industries. Their employees feel a high sense of belonging, resulting in 75% fewer sick days. That's a $2.5 million productivity gain per year for an organization with 10,000 employees.[46]

Conversely, employees who feel excluded have a 50% higher turnover rate. That company with 10,000 employees? Its recruiting and retention costs are soaring by about $10 million per year. But when employees feel they belong, they perform 56% better, a gain of $52 million per year for that company with 10,000 employees.[47]

"There are so many practical strategies that can advance a metaclusive culture in a meaningful way," Higgins notes. "The most important of them focus [on] ways to help each individual feel truly represented, valued, and accepted. They range from big changes—like ensuring your employees, C suite, and board reflect the makeup of your community—to subtler things, like using gender pronouns and participating in community events that your employees value."

The bottom line? Successful organizations flex to recruit and retain more top talent, harness more creativity, and enjoy stronger financials when they are metaclusive. In short, the market rewards them.

Key Learning Points

1. Millennials (Gen Y), Gen X, and Gen Z are on the rise in the American workforce but baby boomers won't go quietly. Organizations that want to be ahead of the disruption curve are using creative strategies to understand generational differences to better attract, recruit, and integrate diverse employees for the good of the firm.

2. The #MeToo movement has shined a bright national spotlight on 100 years of discrimination and sexual harassment experienced by America's working women. Progressive organizations recognize that change—and stronger business performance—starts with female representation at the top, in the C suite and boardroom.

3. Immigrants are the primary engine behind America's economic growth. They're better educated, more innovative, and more likely to be recognized as Nobel laureates than native-born Americans are.

4. Organizations are missing the opportunity to employ talented disabled individuals. They represent the largest group of unemployed Americans. Assistive technology and targeted training can make all the difference.

5. Leading organizations build in rules and systems to remove inherent bias and promote healthy workplaces where diversity can thrive by embracing a multitude of genders, races, sexual orientations, religions, and disabilities. Such firms thrive with lower turnover, fewer sick days, improved performance, and lower recruiting and retention costs.

4 The Way We Work Is Changing

Things may come to those who wait, but only the things left by those who hustle.

Source: Abraham Lincoln

N ow that you understand how and why the newest members of the American workforce are seeking alternatives to their parents' 60-plus-hour work weeks and dedication to climbing the corporate ladder, you can see why our nation's "gig economy" is growing at an unprecedented rate. The gig economy, of course, refers to the plethora of short-term and freelance ventures ballooning around the globe.

Thanks to the gig economy, you can catch an Uber ride in a Corvette driven by a local retiree, get an "influencer's" review of everything from makeup to bicycles via YouTube before you buy, or hire an independent language tutor to chat with on Skype. And that's just the tip of the iceberg.

You can find someone to assemble your Ikea bookshelf via TaskRabbit, recruit a designer for your business card on Fiverr, or make a reservation with someone renting a room on Airbnb. The gig economy is making it possible for individuals everywhere to earn an income in exchange for sharing their skill set.

Said another way, each of these individuals trades his or her time for a set fee in a direct contract with someone who needs a service. Companies are mainly cut out of the middle. Many giggers find safety in the opportunity for multiple income streams.

Remember our previous discussion of transaction costs with Professor Cocron in Chapter 2? He said that companies exist to absorb the overhead that's required to recruit, train, and negotiate with employees. Well, in the gig economy, entrepreneurs are disrupting all that by outcompeting those companies. In many cities, you'll get a cheaper, better ride with Uber than you will in a taxi.

And the gig economy is *exploding* today. Not just in the United States, but worldwide. Our neighbors to the north in Canada are embracing the concept in droves, with more than 40% of millennials participating in the gig economy over the past five years.[1] In the US, the concept first gathered serious steam during the Great Recession in 2008–2009 when the economy shed more than 8.7 million jobs.[2] And it has only grown since then.

Today, more than one-third of Americans report that they are participating in one way or another, with 49% of adults under 35 gigging it.[3] According to one Florida report,[4] gig workers tend to be slightly more educated than other US workers, are more likely to live in an urban area, and are younger (with 43% of them age 25 to 34).

And, for all the criticism that the gig economy takes advantage of freelancers by asking them to work without traditional employment benefits, one aspect that is often overlooked is that the gig economy is truly a champion of diversity. The nature of the gig business is ruthless in cutting through bureaucratic red tape to directly and specifically ensure that customers get what they are looking for: a specific skill to get the job done. In other words, the gig goes to the best-qualified applicant for the price, irrespective of location, gender, age, or background. It is market driven, and that's a beautiful thing.

These individuals view gig work as an opportunity to build new skills, get a career start, and as a pathway to entrepreneurship. Some see gigs as a potential entrée into full-time job opportunities. And, when the recent COVID-19 pandemic resulted in historic levels of unemployment—leaving 20.5 million unemployed by May 2020[5]— the gig economy was a blessing for many.

The Number-One Thing Gig Workers Want

The biggest things to keep in mind as you compete for Gen X, Y, and Z workers in the gig economy? Work–life integration! It's what next-gen workers crave *most* in a job. In one survey,[6] nearly 17% of respondents said it was the most important factor they consider when choosing a job . . . more than leadership opportunities, flexibility, professional development, and a laundry list of other benefits.

This is a particular area of concern for two-career couples. Just like Tom, my millennial associate who told me he wasn't interested in long hours or a fast track to making partner at our firm because his wife's career took precedence in their family, millions of couples are struggling with how to best balance dual careers. According to the Bureau of Labor Statistics, this is true for nearly half of American couples and 63% of couples with kids.[7]

They want to know: How can I be my best self at work while also meeting my family obligations and stay connected to my spouse? The most successful view themselves as a team—partners in navigating their individual challenges together—rather than competitors for time and resources.

They are able to say no to work requests for the good of the family and negotiate career expectations together. Does your organization recognize this reality for your employees? How will you help them succeed?

As we've discussed, it isn't really about the idea of work–life *balance* for these up and comers; it's about work–life *integration*. And that looks a bit different. Because if we are just talking about the opportunity to cut down on commute time with telecommuting, we've recently run that experiment and it isn't all it was cracked up to be.

In spring 2020, for the first time in the history of America, everyone who was not deemed to be an essential worker by the government was suddenly working from home during the height of the COVID-19 pandemic. In fact, pre-pandemic—in January 2020—just 3% of workers were remote. That soared to 64% just three months later.[8] And that experiment demonstrated some surprising results.

The first surprise for many employers who'd been reluctant to allow workers to telecommute was that productivity actually soared. Although they began by telling telecommuters they'd be keeping a close eye on productivity, it soon became clear that work was bleeding into evening hours and weekends for pretty much everyone. In fact, for example, the 53,000 workers suddenly telecommuting at the Social Security Administration registered an 11% improvement in the backlog of pending cases in less than two months of working from home.[9] This, of course, presented its own challenges for employers whose workers were supposed to be "off the clock" when their normal workday ended.

Is remote work here to stay in a big way? That remains to be seen. Employers who rent lots of office space are looking around and wondering if they really need it. Concepts like hoteling—where remote workers share on-site office space by reserving a desk—may see an increase in popularity.

However comfortable the pandemic workday may have been during stay-at-home orders, many were also antsy to get back to the office. The structure so many of us relied on was missing. We realized for the first time that "drive time" was a welcome opportunity to plan our workday on the way to the office and to decompress on the way home from work.

With no structure, it just seemed easier to work on clearing our email inbox before bed; there was just no escape from the world of work. But as you will see, the notion of shutting down and recharging, no matter how brief, remains important, even as we move toward more work–life integration.

When working from home is done well, psychologists emphasize that it can improve employee productivity, creativity, and morale. For certain types of workers—those who need to focus deeply and don't require a lot of collaboration or social support, for example, telecommuting can eliminate distractions and interruptions that affect performance.

Plus, it confers benefits to classes of workers who otherwise face discrimination when working from the office. That single mom who leaves early to pick up her child from day care? She's less likely to be passed over for promotions when working from home. Instead of getting the side eye from coworkers who suspect she's working less than they are, her quality job performance can speak for itself.

The same holds true for disabled workers who may be discriminated against when working at the office. At home, their disabilities are invisible, finally putting them on par with their coworkers when judged by actual job performance. Working from home can be an excellent way to reduce or eliminate the unconscious bias of workplace discrimination.

However, as most experts agree, there is no substitute for face-to-face interaction or "management by walking around." Body language and eye contact are hugely beneficial in the world of work. So is the opportunity for supervisors to interact spontaneously and in-person with workers. Some of the very best innovations occur because someone thought to stop by a coworker's desk on her way to or from a meeting with a great idea.

Throughout my career, I've had the habit of walking around the office to see who was available when I was ready to assign a project to a new associate. I also make a point of traveling to meet new colleagues in our firm or to spend time with clients, because I know there's no substitute for making a personal connection when it comes to work. Zoom or texting can never replace that.

There is great value in being physically visible at work for spontaneous, informal conversations, with both your supervisor and your coworkers. Offsite retreats, company picnics, and "icebreaker" exercises for teams have always worked as ways for people who work together to spend time together and learn to care about each other. Those activities improve loyalty, retention, and cultivate a cohesive team.

So, although the COVID-19 pandemic may have sped up the transition of more work-from-home arrangements, organizations that flex will think longer term as they weigh the trade-offs between what's good for the company and what's good for the worker. In some cases, maybe there is an opportunity to disrupt industries moving remotely with new ways of facilitating in-person engagement and interaction.

Face time—the old-fashioned kind—still matters.

Work–Life Integration Still Requires Time Off

Burnout is ravaging the American workforce. Even the World Health Organization has recognized it as a worrisome syndrome linked to workplace stress that hasn't been well managed. In one study, half of workers—44% of men and 46% of women[10]—said they feel burnout at work. The numbers are even higher for workers with longer tenure at a job. Does this surprise you? Two weeks of paid time off is something many in the US aspire to.

But workers in other countries would never stand for such a paltry amount of time off. Just consider member countries of the European Union, which mandates a minimum of 20 days of annual leave . . . and that doesn't include the generous number of paid holidays. Spain has 14 public holidays. Austria and Germany have 13. Workers in some lucky European countries enjoy up to 38 paid holidays altogether![11]

To beat the pervasive burnout that is ravaging corporate America, it requires more than just less time at the office. In fact, nearly half of workers feel burned out at work.[12] True work–life integration requires time to enjoy life and de-stress, whether that means beach time on a Greek Island or a local day hike. Unfortunately, that's becoming harder and harder for Americans to do. Even if you do fly all the way to that remote Greek island, you'll likely be looking for a hotel with a strong Wi-Fi signal so you can check email. This is the challenge of work–life integration.

Although you may be physically absent from the office, it's very likely that your boss still expects you to keep in touch by email. And it's not just a problem with the boss. The reality is that most of us, as workers, have become addicted to the 24/7 culture of work and are not so great at unplugging.

I confess I'm guilty. Throughout my career, I've always taken pride in the fact that I was easy to reach . . . never far from a phone or computer. (Under the guise of "hiking" on a vacation in Puerto Rico one year, I convinced my daughter to accompany me up a steep mountain in search of a cell signal.) But being ever reachable just might be an outdated notion. In fact, it's far more common among professionals of my generation than it is among those coming up in the world of work.

Is it fair for me to hold younger workers to the same standard if they are able to perform better by periodically "recharging their batteries"? Employers would do well to remember that work–life integration isn't about *always* being available, it's about maintaining control over when you're available. The key is the opportunity to compartmentalize. In other words, it's fine to carve out time for checking your email while on vacation to stay in touch with the office, but it's also restorative to put your computer away for hours—or days—at a time. That's integration at its best.

Legal Changes Are Brewing

Although the gig economy appears here to stay, all is not rosy in this new era of flexible working arrangements. There's increasing tension on all fronts as America works to come to a common understanding of what it really means to be an employee. Recent legal challenges strike at the very heart of this model.

In a May 2018 decision by the California Supreme Court,[13] the court ruled in favor of placing the burden on employers to prove workers are *not* employees. The lawsuit was brought by a Los Angeles–based transportation service against Uber, who claimed the rideshare service was undercutting its competition by misclassifying workers as independent contractors, thereby shaving $500 million of annual transaction costs in California alone by avoiding payment of benefits such as health care, unemployment insurances, overtime, and minimum wage.[14] And the court agreed.

The crux of the question was whether Uber exerted enough control over workers that it should reasonably classify them as employees. And that's a thorny legal issue. Even the IRS and Department of Labor—not to mention state labor boards—use different tests and standards to gauge whether independent contractor status is appropriate. The IRS considers more than 20 different factors that range from behavioral and financial control to the relationship between the employer and worker to make its decision.[15]

As a consequence of the legal challenge, the state of California issued some guidance on this topic in late 2019[16] with some serious restrictions on who can be hired and for how many hours before freelancers must be deemed employees. That ruling, however, could put the brakes on a whole host of companies that rely on independent contractors in the nation's gig economy.

As media companies rushed to end freelance writer contracts in favor of hiring part-time employees, the ruling had the unintended consequence of potentially devastating the livelihood of the state's freelance writers and photographers. As of this writing, similar lawsuits were pending against DoorDash and Instacart.

And it could trigger a whole host of other lawsuits under California's Assembly Bill 5 law, which allows individuals to sue companies over labor violations on behalf of the state. New Jersey, Massachusetts, and Connecticut use a similar litmus test to AB5, which could make companies in those states vulnerable, too.[17]

Industry groups representing their interests struck back with a lawsuit of their own, just as a professional association for truck drivers had done shortly before them. And although the truckers won a temporary reprieve from the law, a federal court denied a restraining order that would've blocked the law from taking effect against the writers.

For better or for worse, more new laws and regulations are coming to the gig economy. The reality is that American labor and employment laws were designed to support a pre-internet workforce and are now far outdated. That status quo cannot endure in light of the ways in which work is changing. In a nod to the changing world of work, even the US Congress included gig workers (with some exclusions) for the first time as beneficiaries of its COVID-19 stimulus package.

That's likely due to the fact that Congress had already been studying the role of the gig economy within the larger context of trends affecting the future of work. As you might anticipate, the views of legislators vary widely. On the one hand, Democrats are focused on the rights of independent workers and favor legislation that grants them minimum wage, overtime pay protections, the opportunity to unionize, and creates eligibility for workers' compensation and unemployment insurance benefits.

On the other hand, Republicans are aiming for a compromise approach. As Rep. Tim Walberg (R-MI) summarized their position, "Instead of considering unworkable policies that will harm workers and businesses, we should be discussing ways to encourage flexible work arrangements and access to employer-sponsored benefits without creating costly and restrictive mandates."[18]

Even recent presidential hopefuls waded in with plans. Self-styled Democratic-Socialist Bernie Sanders (I-VT), for instance, released a comprehensive plan for "workplace democracy" to actually crack down on the gig economy, which—as he sees it—exploits workers.

Meanwhile, the Hamilton Project, a think tank within the Brookings Institution, is looking ahead with its proposal of a new classification of "independent worker," which is essentially a hybrid between a traditional employee and independent contractor. In this scenario, the employer would still exert some control over the means and methods of work, but not as much as traditionally with employees.

In a major development that could serve as model for other states around the country struggling with the classification of gig workers, California voters, in November 2020, approved Proposition 22 to preserve the independent contractor status of rideshare and delivery drivers.

The trade? The new law also requires the gig companies to pay at least 120 percent minimum wage as well as health care subsidies and reimbursement for gas and wear-and-tear and enter into written agreements with their workers to ensure they are not terminated except for reasons enumerated in a written contract. Strict antidiscrimination and antiharassment policies will be enforced, along with safety training.[19]

It seems likely that America will continue to debate the finer details of worker protections versus freedom and flexibility in the gig economy for some time to come.

The Gig Boom Is Disrupting Business as Usual

Plenty of industries are being disrupted by the new gig economy, too. In one downtown San Francisco hotel, the room service staff increasingly finds itself delivering far more empty dishes and glasses than actual meals as guests order out through Door Dash and UberEATS. Hotel guests are checking restaurants on Yelp instead of chatting with the concierge and hailing a Lyft rather than asking the bellhop to call a cab.[20]

Gig workers are also flocking to health care, as nurses, ambulance drivers, and pharmacists each embrace the freedom of flexible contracts. Gigs for physical and occupational therapy services and specialized imaging services confer benefits to hospital employers as well as workers because they can better flex according to demand.

But, does it make sense to invest time and training into temporary workers? Is it really possible to create cohesiveness and loyalty in a team with too many people joining and leaving the gig? Even before the gig economy, hospitals have struggled with these issues as they've hired temporary traveling nurses to fill in for full-time nursing staff during shortages and recruitment challenges. Their experience is that a loyal, retained workforce will always deliver higher quality for a lower cost. So time will tell.

As you can see, the gig economy represents one more gigantic shift in the world of work with both winners and losers, disruptors and disrupted. For people with skills who are unemployed or need flex time due to other commitments, it's a boon.

More Than a Side Hustle

One of the things that makes it challenging to identify workable legislative or regulatory solutions is that the gig economy attracts a broad range of workers with differing needs and goals. For some, the gig is a part-time job in which workers moonlight to supplement and support other money-making efforts.

For others, that couldn't be further from the truth. Just consider bloggers and other influencers who have hatched a robust industry by converting social media followers to customers for brands they endorse through product promotion.

What began a decade ago as charismatic millennials sharing favorite recipes and diary-style reflections online has morphed into a profitable quest for eyeballs on posts. In 1999, there were just 23 blogs on the internet. Today, there are 512 *million* of them![21]

Some full-time "digital nomads" spend their days carefully crafting blog posts that are optimized for search engines so they pop to the top of page 1 of Google. Then they capture affiliate income when readers buy on Amazon or reserve hotels through Booking.com. One 33-year-old dad and entrepreneur traded his day job as a college admissions counselor for a full-time online fashion design business made possible through his 10-year men's style blog.[22]

Consider this: the top 10 YouTube influencers in 2018 earned $180 million.[23] So don't kid yourself . . . this is not navel-gazing by hobby publishers; this is the intentional construction of sophisticated online businesses with multiple income streams.

What About Benefits and Health Care?

One of the biggest challenges of the gig economy is the fact that health care is employer-based in the United States. Although employer-sponsored health care may seem normal to Americans—because "that's how it's always been"—it's far from usual in the rest of the world. In Europe, for example, every citizen is automatically enrolled in a national health care system run by the government where the great majority of care is provided for "free." (Assuming, of course, that you discount the increased tax burden on citizens.)

So why is this basic human right that is enjoyed by most industrialized nations dependent on employment here in the US? After all, we still get sick if we are laid off a job, are looking to change jobs, or need to take time off to care for a child or elderly parent. The answer may surprise you: it's a relic left over from World War II and postwar America.

The Kaiser Shipyards, owned by Henry Kaiser, began the practice in the 1940s. As Kaiser's West Coast shipyard operation swelled in response to huge orders for merchant ships, workers nationwide flocked to the operation eager for employment. To fill the huge need for housing, Kaiser built housing units in Portland, Oregon, also establishing local social and health care services for these workers.[24] This enabled an offset for wage freezes suffered by employees during the war and a way to compete for talent when the labor market tightened after the GIs returned. It was the foundation of the Kaiser Permanente health care system that exists today.

And that link between employment and the provision of health care first established almost 80 years ago still endures all these years later as a prominent and often unfortunate reality of American life today, even though for-profit companies are not in the social services business and this model arguably limits American socioeconomic mobility.

It's worth noting that some predict the COVID pandemic will create a new groundswell of support for the idea that health care is a right rather than a luxury. Even the US government said it would pay for uninsured patients to get COVID-19 testing.[25] UnitedHealthcare, one of the nation's largest insurers, which previously opted out of the Affordable Care Act's health exchanges, has opted back in.[26] With so many Americans losing employment during the pandemic, it's become clear to them that employer-based care is just plain risky with catastrophic rates of unemployment.

In some ways, the American dream is more alive in Nordic countries where they better support the kind of opportunity, freedom, and independence cherished by Americans. The Swedes, for example, view personal control through *protection* against risk, and Americans view control as *taking* risks. The Swedish government provides nine months of parental leave to be shared between parents and a taxpayer-funded health care system,[27] whereas the US struggles politically to reach consensus on any paid leave program.

And yet, the US spends nearly twice as much on health care than other wealthy industrialized nations, with the lowest life expectancy, highest suicide rate, and largest chronic disease burden.[28] How will we fix this troubled system?

Although some form of national health care is viewed as socialism—synonymous somehow with the loss of freedom—the pros and cons are, of course, far more complex and nuanced than we can do justice to in a few pages here, but they merit at least a brief consideration.

For one thing, it's worth noting that American concerns about wait times, substandard care, and government control are frequently overstated and don't hold up to the actual realities in nations with universal health care. Likewise, the huge benefits of such health care systems are often understated in American discussions about effective ways to improve health care for the majority while reducing the overall cost burden.

When the government can bulk-buy equipment and services directly, it cuts out the extra cost of health insurers as brokers and gains substantial cost efficiencies and administrative efficiencies. Plus, some countries overlay options for access to private specialists and hospitals for additional cost onto public health options.

In many cases, it's the best of both worlds: preventive care and life-saving surgeries are available to everyone, while those with means can access top-tier specialists and services on their own. And, really, it's not so different from how older Americans already access American health care: the government pays for basic care through Medicare with supplemental coverage available through the American Association of Retired Persons (AARP) and other sources. That's where the slogan "Medicare for All" came from.

Higher Spending for Worse Outcomes

Other wealthy industrialized nations spend just half as much per person on health care as the US spends.[29] There are lots of complex economic, political, and social characteristics that make it challenging for direct comparisons here, but it's worth noting that the spending gap between the US and comparable countries continues to widen.[30]

One of those reasons may be because of the overuse of services in the US that do not correlate with higher quality. As Atul Gawande, MD, MPH, points out in his excellent *New Yorker* article, "The Cost Conundrum," more care is not necessarily better care . . . and sometimes it's actually *worse* care. He says we are currently in a battle for the "soul of American medicine."[31]

Gawande has crunched the Medicare data by US region and found that patients in regions where doctors spend more on tests and treatments actually have worse or similar outcomes to patients in regions where doctors spend far less. That's because extra tests, hospital stays, and medicines also bring extra risks.

Why would doctors order too many tests and treatments, you're wondering? One reason, according to Gawande, is that some physicians are focused on improving revenue streams of their practices. We're paying them based on quantity rather than quality. Because American physicians are frequently self-employed and contract with hospitals (unlike, say, European doctors who are in part paid by the government), they must watch the bottom line just like any other business.

Just like other businesses, doctors can become focused on improving income streams from profitable work and minimizing time on less profitable work. Oncologists make money on chemotherapy treatments. Rheumatologists offer in-office infusions of biologic treatments when there are frequently other less costly medications patients can administer at home. It can be a conflict of interest.

Is this *fraud*? Occasionally it is, but more frequently, it's the predictable result of mixing for-profit business and medicine in the US today. Patients become potential profit centers.

And yet, the advent of not-for-profit accountable care organizations is changing this in some regions. For instance, the Mayo Clinic in Rochester, Minnesota, disincentivizes these practices quite intentionally—and successfully I might add—through salaries and collaboration.

One of the communities with the lowest health care costs in the nation is Grand Junction, Colorado. Their secret? An agreement among physicians not to cherry-pick profitable patients and a peer review committee dedicated to rooting out unnecessary procedures and reducing hospital complication rates.

There's really no question that our current health care system is not sustainable. It's not meeting the needs of its citizens and costs are a runaway train. And, as Gawande notes, it's perhaps true that there is extra fat in the system . . . that we *can* cut out costs without sacrificing outcomes in just the way other countries with universal health care have done.

One expert[32] suggests Medicare could save 30% without sacrificing quality by focusing on the opportunity to bring regions that are overusing health care into alignment with those that are medium and low users.[33]

Perhaps, as Gawande suggests, we are ultimately asking the wrong question when thinking about the choice between our current system and European-style universal health care. Maybe fixing the system is less about *who* pays for care and more about making *somebody* accountable for *results* based on the total care delivered, both quality and cost with appropriate penalties and incentives.

The good news: as the world of work continues to shift, the need for our current health care system to align with it becomes ever more obvious, creating increasing pressure for change. Against all odds and much resistance, the Affordable Care Act (ACA)—otherwise known as Obamacare—was signed into law by President Barack Obama in 2010, creating important new protections for Americans.

And although we can debate whether it was rushed and failed to achieve bi-partisan support and is therefore flawed, it is not debatable that it moved the needle toward much needed health care reform. Consider that millennials can now retain their parents' insurance up until age 26. And, the introduction of state health exchanges allows individuals without employer-sponsored health care to purchase insurance for the first time ever.

Heck, even health insurance companies flocked back to the ACA's state health care exchanges in the wake of the COVID-19 pandemic.[34] Early on, they fled the exchanges, fearing losses from covering too many sick people. How quickly things change. With record unemployment during the pandemic, job-based coverage became shaky. By comparison, the ACA's partially government-subsidized care looks stable. Plus, a recent study by the Kaiser Family Foundation[35] showed insurers' fears were largely unfounded. Insurers seeing ACA patients performed just fine.

Although the US has a long way to go toward shaping a national health care policy and system with better outcomes for lower costs that other nations enjoy, the ACA was a significant first step. And, more recently, hospital reimbursement is becoming linked to quality improvement targets (such as fewer medical errors) and cost reduction. Other experiments are underway too as employers look for ways to reduce the increasing cost burden of providing health care to their employees.

One of these experiments is an uptick in interest of "centers of excellence." Under this model, employers contract directly with health care organizations who meet certain quality benchmarks and then negotiate a discount for a volume of specialized procedures; for example, Walmart would contract all heart surgeries through the Cleveland Clinic (a fictional example for edification here).

The big surprise? The centers of excellence model is catching on but not because the negotiated discount saves money on procedures that employees undergo. Rather, this model requires individuals to obtain a second opinion at the center of excellence *after* they consult a local specialist before they undergo a procedure.

So where these centers of excellence are really saving money is through their reluctance to recommend unnecessary, invasive procedures that add costs and can worsen outcomes. That's because the center's standards often require a clinical consensus from an accredited board of advisors.

"Ultimately, the centers of excellence are effective because they standardize care. And standardized care in medicine lowers costs and raises quality," explains Stephen Trzeciak MD, affiliated with Cooper University Health System in Camden, New Jersey and Anthony Mazzarelli MD, co-president and CEO of the Health System, and authors of *Compassionomics: The Revolutionary Scientific Evidence That Caring Makes a Difference.*[36] Because Cooper is itself a center of excellence, the authors have seen firsthand the difference it makes in both quality outcomes for patients and lower costs.

The centers for excellence approach also hints at another experiment in reinventing medicine that is underway in America: the value of standardization. In another *New Yorker* article,[37] also by Atul Gawande some years ago, "Big Med," Gawande wonders about the striking lack of standardization in medicine.

He marvels at the ability of the Cheesecake Factory restaurant to deliver a diverse menu of food items—more than 600 choices—with consistently excellent quality while the average hospital visit is typically a confusing experience with poor communication, lack of coordination among specialists, and variable results depending on the choices of the treating physician. Surely, an individual receiving medical care for pneumonia in the emergency room deserves at least the same level of care and attention a skilled chef offers for a fine meal.

Gawande makes a compelling case for delivering higher quality and lower cost by putting patients at the center of their care—in the same way restaurants do—rather than at the periphery, dependent on the whims and convenience of treatment providers, as it works in American health care today.

Standardized care protocols can help here. Around the country, in an experiment with "Big Medicine," large corporate health systems are mandating the use of specific protocols for all physicians to use based on cost and quality. And those experiments are succeeding and delivering faster, better results for patients at a lower cost. However, as Gawande also notes, America is not great at scaling good ideas that work, which may account for why we're not seeing more widespread innovation of the kinds he cited back in his 2012 article.

Even if Big Medicine can succeed, it will have plenty of political obstacles to overcome. To fully embrace its potential, liberals would have to accept the idea of a continuing market based approach to health care. Conservatives would have to accept strong governmental oversight. These are challenging notions in hyper-partisan America.

Portable Benefits Seem Imminent

One of the more recent developments to support the gig economy seems to be bipartisan interest in new legislation that would allow portable benefits to benefit both employers and gig workers.

Under such a plan, independent workers would be able to carry benefits such as sick time, paid days off, medical insurance, 401K plans, and other typical employment benefits from one job to another as often as they switch employers. The idea represents another giant step forward in the retooling of benefits that match the boom in this alternative workforce.

And states are taking the lead here over the federal government. The State of California set things in motion in fall 2019 when it adopted this kind of safety net in Assembly Bill 5 for Uber and Lyft drivers.[38] Shortly thereafter, the city of Philadelphia became the first city nationwide to create a portable bank of paid time off (PTO) for domestic workers, potentially creating a blueprint for the gig economy in the rest of the country.[39] Under the plan, eligible workers accrue one hour of paid time off for every 40 hours worked. Employers contribute a prorated amount of the worker's PTO bank based on the worker's pay.

At press time, New Jersey was expected to pass Senate Bill 943 to a wider group of gig workers by requiring companies who contract with at least 50 independent workers to contribute funds for them to a qualified benefit provider over a 12-month period.[40] Washington State, which introduced a similar measure, is also, of course, home to Seattle, one of the few locations in the country—along with New York City—to also pass minimum wage legislation for ride-share drivers.[41]

Flex or Be Disrupted

Now that you understand your competition in the gig economy and how health care and other benefits are innovating to support those changes, it's time to think about how your organization can do a better job of recruiting those workers.

If you don't want to follow in the footsteps of the hospitality industry—bleeding jobs as user-friendly apps take over for real people—consider flexing now to offer the kinds of benefits workers are embracing in the gig economy to better compete for talent.

Remember that many of those who are swapping out full-time employment for gigs are doing so because they're in search of perks such as setting their own schedule and working remotely. Can you offer that?

If so, your organization might win out over the appeal of gigs. As we discussed, Gen Z also craves team collaboration, leadership opportunities, meaning in their work, and professional development. Many corporations may have a leg up here, too.

Have you considered using more independent workers instead of hiring more full-time employees? The gig economy is a rich source of talent that's ripe for recruiting by the right company. In one survey,[42] companies who used independent workers said they liked the ability to flex capacity as needed and also gain access to more specialized skills. They also said independent workers were more cost-efficient and more productive.

Before you jump in, though, do a thorough review of the current rules and regulations for employees versus freelancers to examine disparities and be sure to reduce key legal exposures. As one human resources executive notes, there is a fundamental misalignment between the leading practices many use for their permanent employees and the ones they use for independent workers.[43]

Another question to consider: Does your organization view free-lancers as temporary workers who are disposable? Are they less worthy of the consideration you offer regular employees in some way? Those are dated attitudes favored by companies that become disrupted.

From a legal standpoint, the challenge for employers is to take appropriate steps to ensure employees and gig workers are clearly distinct. You should embrace them as valued contributors to your organization, provide access to information to help them do their jobs, and encourage cross-collaboration. However, too many blurred lines can be an invitation for lawsuits as noted previously in our discussion of Uber.

Make sure that the worker is truly independent by clearly defining the terms of the gig. Use a written agreement where possible to define the scope of the project. Make it clear that the worker is free to com-plete the project on his or her time and, reasonably, in the manner he or she choose.

Remember, these workers are not employees, which is why many freely chose this path. The more you treat the independent worker like an employee—and that worker *acts* like an employee—the more likely he or she could be legally considered an employee and to be entitled to all that comes with that status. To avoid blurring that line, resist the impulse to control the *when, where*, and *how* an independent contrac-tor performs the job.

Maintain a big-picture view of your whole workforce. Even though freelancers may work on a transactional or project basis, shift your leadership style to strategic and collaborative management. Are your HR policies designed to create an overall positive experience? Most workers love feedback and younger workers in particular value technology so take advantage of both when reaching into the gig economy.

Make onboarding, project workflow, and information sharing effortless. Recognize their contributions and encourage their feedback and ideas. Ultimately the gig worker might decide to become a full-time employee of your organization. Don't turn away from an opportunity to recruit this talent.

As the corporate ladder collapses in the face of Gen X, Y, and Z preferences, think about it as a lattice instead. Ask: How can we foster a spirit of entrepreneurship in the organization? How can we identify ways to allow employees to zigzag their way in a career with opportunities for creativity, flexibility, and collaboration depending on their professional interests and personal preferences?

Also, don't skimp on cybersecurity training for gig workers. Although lawsuits to date have focused on classification and protection of workers, this is likely to be the next legal flashpoint. Why? The unique, flexible affiliation between companies and gig workers can leave a company far more vulnerable to resulting breaches.

If gig workers have the same access to your company's information that traditional employees do, a click on an unsafe email, downloading an unverified file, or not maintaining current security updates can quickly lead to a data breach.

Training and auditing can reduce those risks, but be sure to work with legal counsel to implement a training program that doesn't veer too far into the employment path, too. In the same way that you limit electronic access to information among employees, you must also thoughtfully limit gig workers' access. Because they often work remotely, it can be easy to overlook threats posted by your external communications where they may access and store company information on their own devices. These and other privacy issues are becoming more and more apparent as we advance technologically.

One other important legal exposure to consider: workplace safety. Because the gig economy tends to attract younger workers, those workers may have minimal work history and less experience with occupational safety hazards. When you put those two things in the context of high-risk industries—for example, passenger transportation and freight delivery services—you're looking at a whole host of areas where you may be legally exposed.

That's why the gig economy can trigger the agenda of the Occupational Safety and Health Administration (OSHA) to reduce workplace violence. In other words, OSHA expects you, as a company using gig workers, to protect them from safety threats.

In many cases, gig workers are performing in-home projects or transportation for complete strangers. This exposure to the public makes violence-related issues a recognized safety concern. It's just a matter of time before aggressive plaintiffs' attorneys find a viable way to hold companies liable for these kinds of injuries.

So, the markers of today's disruptive companies successfully tapping the gig economy? Progressive human resources policies. Robust worker protections and benefits. And a true strategic partnership mind-set.

Excel in these areas and gig workers are yours for the taking.

Key Learning Points

1. More than one-third of Americans currently work in the gig economy, making it a robust source of talent for disruptive organizations to recruit talent. The gig economy is also disrupting industries in unprecedented ways as some organizations get left behind.

2. The number-one thing gig workers want in a job is work–life integration. This is particularly true of Gen X, Y, and Z workers because it's a core value.

3. Health care and other benefits of traditional employment have not yet caught up to the gig economy. However, recent state legislation offers a compelling preview of what's to come—such as portable benefits—as the rights and responsibilities of both employers and workers are reexamined in a new era. Even the US Congress is beginning to weigh in.

4. Companies who flex will embrace the gig economy by offering benefits and opportunities that align with the goals and desires of this rich source of talent, while simultaneously paying attention to the growing legal risks in the employment relationship as well as the protection of personal information.

5 The Tools of Work Are Changing

We change our tools and then our tools change us.

—Source: Jeff Bezos

As a child, Abdullah was told he probably wouldn't make it to age 30 due to his congenital disabilities. He doesn't have hands. In fact, his arms end at the elbow. He's also had a facial and speech deformity since birth. Thanks to medical advancements, however, he is a healthy man in his 30s, one who has beat those odds.

He's also happily employed at Amazon, in Philadelphia, working in warehouse delivery logistics. How did this miracle occur? Abdullah sought out technology and training from The Sierra Group, a Philadelphia-based company that has been "**S**eeking **I**nclusion for **E**veryone **R**equiring **R**easonable **A**ccommodation" since 1992.

With their help, he learned how to use a computer at a workstation that was adapted to fit his unique body and typing style. And thanks to other technology adaptations, and his own creativity, Abdullah drives his own car to work these days, too.

This is just one small way for one segment of America's workers—there are many—that technology is redefining the world of work. The credit for successes like Abdullah's (and thousands of others with diverse disabilities) goes to organizations nationwide, such as The Sierra Group, that are harnessing the advances in assistive technology (AT) and artificial intelligence (AI) in astonishing new ways.

The field has come a long, long way. The Sierra Group should know. The organization has been on the forefront of AT since 1992, pre-Google! Back then, when Eliot Spindel, a young van driver at Eastern Airlines, fell down a set of stairs, broke his neck, and developed C-2 quadriplegia, Sierra set him up with an early version of Dragon-Dictate, a speech recognition package that ultimately put him back to work. After learning how to operate a computer with only the sound of his voice, he was able to complete a computer programming course and went on to work in software development and web design until the age of 65.

These days, of course, all of us are talking to our phones or asking Alexa to lower the lights in our homes. Sierra's CEO Janet D. Fiore is awestruck by the shift. "Back in 1992, in addition to setting up Eliot with DragonDictate for his computer, we also enabled his use of the first speech recognition technology for home automation," she says. "We distributed the Butler in a Box by Mastervoice. It cost $10,000 and when you spoke to it, it would turn on your lights and TV, adjust your thermostat . . . essentially all the things Alexa does today for less than $100. For people like Eliot, this assistive technology made the difference between independence and no independence."[1]

Today, Americans with all kinds of disabilities are enjoying the power of a paycheck, feeling pride in accomplishment, and enjoying new independence that is transforming their lives. AT has exploded around the country, breaking most barriers to employment for those with disabilities. So much so, that state vocational rehab departments routinely include staff and vendors with deep expertise in AT who can overcome just about any kind of work-related impairment.

There's an App for That

People with disabilities are not the only Americans benefiting from technology advancements. Artificial intelligence has opened up new consumer markets far beyond the traditional uses of robotics. From landscaping services to bridal registries, customers are enjoying more choices and better service from the products they want most when they order online.

Walmart is automating the unloading of its trucks while Californian farmers are using robots to harvest lettuce. Breakthrough technology[2] has brought us social networking, the global positioning system (GPS) that navigates our Google Maps, touchscreens, and "no-touch" screens for contactless credit card payments. Android's and Apple's mobile operating systems dominate the world.

During the height of the COVID-19 pandemic, visitors to some Asian countries got a late-night phone call from authorities if their tracking device signaled that they were not adhering to mandatory 14-day quarantines. And contact tracing (first used, albeit less efficiently, by Great Britain in the 1930s to combat the rise of sexually transmitted diseases) went mainstream worldwide. The ensuing debate about privacy versus protection in the use of automated contact tracing heated up accordingly.

In the same vein, the Internet of Things—growing at a breakneck pace in America today—is recording our habits and preferences, automatically starting our car with the authentication of a password or turning on the air conditioning system as we walk in the door at home.

Even in law, my own industry, AI is revolutionizing legal research, document review, and document drafting. It's analyzing contracts and even crafting litigation strategy. Some systems now can answer questions about the law in specific jurisdictions.

In the very near future, AI will be able to answer those questions in multiple jurisdictions, essentially synthesizing complex thoughts to answer questions such as "What are the problems that will result from Brexit and its impact on the British legal system?" Soon, AI systems will even begin to predict the outcomes of lawsuits in ways that humans just can't do, a mindbending innovation.

Will Self-Driving Cars Be the New Normal?

One of the most incredible innovations in AI, one that will ultimately affect us all—for better or worse—is the rise of autonomous vehicles (AVs). They will revolutionize transportation, "creating smart cities where traffic flows . . . are centrally coordinated."[3]

Although Uber was a pioneer of the gig economy, it's also been hemorrhaging money due to the high costs of paying its independent drivers, which is, of course, central to its business model. Uber's competitor Lyft lost $911 million in 2018.[4] The best hope for these companies' bottom lines? You guessed it: AVs. Driverless vehicles are an enticing solution. By replacing human drivers with robotic cars, the company could cut out three-quarters of its costs today.

The widespread use of AVs is still a decade away—companies are tempering their investments and sales forecasting as they ask, "How safe is safe enough?"—but Lyft hopes to add at least some of them to the current fleet of drivers in just five years. Across the nation, the idea of driverless cars is gaining traction. AV took one big leap forward when President Donald Trump signed a 2019 executive order to boost the role of AI in the US by making it a priority in federal research and development efforts.

In Florida, the Sunshine State, a new law went into effect on January 1, 2019, that allows AVs to operate on the roads without anyone behind the wheel. Safety concerns are addressed through several provisions. First, the new law mandates that AV systems must alert humans when there's a system failure. Also, safeguards must be in place to satisfy a "minimal risk condition" position. In other words, autonomous vehicles need to be able to pull over and put on emergency lights.

You know who will benefit to a great degree from self-driving cars? Individuals with disabilities such as Abdullah and Eliot. Today, Abdullah commutes to his job thanks to adaptive technology in his car. But Eliot, and many with disabilities, rely solely on very limited (and expensive) vans for public transportation because his disability precludes him from being able to drive. What if he could just ride to work in a driverless vehicle instead?

Transportation has always been a big barrier to employment and community involvement for those with disabilities. Because the ability to drive and possess a driver's license is, under the American's with Disabilities Act, considered an "essential function" in many jobs, employees and employers lose out when there is no way to reasonably accommodate workers.

But soon, driverless cars may change this. Although the ability to drive may still *be* an essential function of some jobs, it's possible that employers may be asked to allow the use of, or even provide, self-driving vehicles as a form of workplace accommodation.

Just think about the value of a self-driving car for all those aging suburban baby boomers. Today, the loss of driving privileges can precipitate a steep decline in functionality, bring on depression, and become the catalyst for a move to a long-term-care facility. Just imagine the possibilities for independence with driverless cars.

Seniors can remain engaged longer in the workforce and volunteer in the community. It's incredibly exciting!

The way goods are transported is likewise being transformed by AI. Look no further than the trucking industry. In 2015, the American Trucking Association reported a shortage of 48,000 truck drivers.[5] Not only are driver shortages a problem, but trucking companies are saddled with an aging workforce, high employee turnover, and a whole slew of federal and state regulations that limit when and how much their drivers may work.

So, consider the boon of driverless trucks. In the same way that driverless cars are going mainstream, driverless 18-wheeers are already being tested on public roads.[6] During testing, humans are riding along—just in case sensors or computers fail—but autonomous trucking executives say that practice will end shortly.

Similar to other AI innovations, the advent of driverless trucks comes with pros and cons. On the one hand, they are expected to eliminate approximately 300,000 jobs,[7] but not *all* trucking jobs. It's anticipated that driverless trucks will stick mainly to interstate highways, leaving local truck drivers to work on secondary road systems. At least for now.

On the other hand, driverless trucks don't ever take their eyes off the road to look at their phone like so many human drivers do. And when you consider the fact that 9 out of 10 car crashes are caused by human error,[8] that's a welcome improvement. Driverless trucks represent a huge boost to safety on the road.

Plus, traditional trucks typically use only 40% of their capacity due to regulations about the number of consecutive hours drivers can drive. But driverless trucks can operate 24 hours per day. That means they can haul the same amount of freight with 40% fewer trucks on the road. And that's great news for reducing traffic congestion, something we can all get behind.

There are also plenty of welcome downstream effects from this sea change coming to the trucking industry. Delivery speeds will increase, which may change ordering patterns, lead times, and inventory levels. It could lead to price reductions, too. After all, transportation costs make up a big part of the price of a product, so if those costs go down, companies could afford to offer more competitive prices.[9]

Even Tesla's getting in on the action. Elon Musk plans to launch his electric cyber truck in 2021 for under $50,000 with a range of between 300 and 500 miles.[10] The cyber truck is brimming with cameras, radars, sensors, and other technology-based features. It's easy to glimpse the future here: it clearly won't be long before Tesla can provide companies with a 24/7 robotic delivery workforce.

In fact, since 2016, a lobby group called the "Self-Driving Coalition for Safer Streets" that includes Google, Volvo, Ford, Uber, and Lyft has been pressing its case among regulators, lawmakers, and local governments.[11] It's headed up by a former chief of the National Highway Traffic Safety Administration.

As you might imagine, all these driverless vehicles will also have a profound effect on the demand for labor in driving-related occupations. In the same way that other jobs are evaporating in the face of technology and automation—as we've seen—truck drivers, bus drivers, electricians, and emergency medical technicians are also increasingly out of work. And, because they tend to be older and less educated self-employed men, the shift to autonomous vehicles will have an outsized negative impact on this segment of the population.[12]

Not only that, but these workers are also less likely to be covered by a pension plan or benefit from employer-sponsored health insurance. That's a real problem because 15.5 million US workers are likely to be affected.[13] Retraining and new opportunities for these displaced workers will be critical. The good news is, for safety and other reasons, human involvement may always be a necessity when it comes to autonomous vehicles and maybe in many other jobs affected by AI. One day soon, maybe those displaced drivers will remotely run an entire fleet.

The bottom line is that now is the time for employers to plan their transition to the world of AV so they can ensure a smooth transition for affected workers. Be aware that legal protections for transit labor—such as trucking, busing, airlines, and shipping companies—already exist in many collective bargaining agreements and under certain federal and state laws. And, mass layoffs or closings may require advance notice to employees.

So, whether you have a unionized workforce or not, it's important to review a variety of labor laws to be sure you are in compliance with all the terms and conditions of employment that will inevitably be affected by your move to AV or other forms of automation.[14]

AI Is Changing Supply Chains, Too

Just as driverless trucks are speeding up product delivery, AI is also revolutionizing the American shopping experience. Just consider Amazon's giant leaps in innovation: technology is at the very core of its ability to fulfill its promise to customers of lightning-fast delivery. Because of its massive sales volume, robots are central to Amazon's two-day delivery model. In fact, more than 200,000 robots work alongside humans in their warehouses today.[15]

In its fulfillment centers, the company can control the speed and direction of robots collecting items for customers. Because it's all about increasing efficiency, tiny gains in time savings result in big increases in profit with each AI innovation. For example, Amazon's new advanced computer vision and machine learning technology frees up human hands from bar coding as items arrive at the warehouse from manufacturers.

At its new "grab-and-go" retail stores, Amazon customers scan their phones to pay for merchandise. There are no checkout counters here. Rather, machine-learning—combined with sensors and cameras—determine when a transaction is complete so that the customer's account can be directly charged.[16]

No interaction required: customers just walk in, select their items, and leave. The goal? To make the consumer experience seamless. Just as online customers click to order and see a box show up at their doorstep (sometimes on the same day as the order was placed), Amazon's retail customers are able to skip the crowded wait in line. How appropriate for our post-pandemic world.

With shopping experiences like this, it's no surprise that traditional brick-and-mortar retail outlets are shuttering. There's just no competition with the likes of Amazon and other organizations harnessing the power of artificial intelligence in service of both customers and profits.

As you can see, AI is reshaping the business landscape in powerful new ways. With an onslaught of new apps connecting users and sellers of services and faster product delivery times, it's good news for American consumers. But the impact of AI doesn't stop there. It's also changing the way that Americans secure employment and are evaluated on job performance.

Robots: The New Gatekeepers

In the old days, humans used to be the gatekeepers for applicants looking to secure a new job. A human resources executive would screen applicant résumés and send the most promising of them on to the hiring manager for review. That manager would choose several candidates for a personal interview, maybe including a few of the applicant's potential coworkers, and then select the best candidate based on a complex set of judgment calls on personality, qualifications, salary requirements, and more. Can a computer really do all of that?

According to LinkedIn,[17] talent acquisition increasingly relies on artificial intelligence to do some of the tedious sifting through résumés, scheduling interviews, and even scoring applicants on aspects of an interview that, up until now, recently seemed better accomplished by humans. Vodaphone, for example, uses AI technology to consider more than 25,000 data points in video interviews that applicants send. It analyzes everything from facial cues to speech cadence.

One recruiting technology firm, HireVue, uses the applicants' own computer and cellphone camera to analyze word choice, speaking voice, and facial movements before ranking them against other potential candidates for a final employability score. This is not some fringe hiring practice, either. It's used so frequently in finance and hospitality industries—with more than a million job seekers analyzed to date—that universities actually train their students how to ace the AI "exam."[18]

But *is* there a "perfect" employee? Can we each be reduced to a composite score based on the tone of our voice and the words we choose? Although some deride this approach as the dark side of technology, others believe that such algorithms eliminate bias in flawed and subjective metrics long used by recruiters who are human. However, some suspect hiring algorithms might actually *create* new bias.[19] Hiring has always been more art than science . . . until now. Stay tuned to see if AI delivers net gains or losses here.

Tracking Your Productivity

We've discussed Amazon's commitment to technology and use of robots at length already. But it also extends to human employees. If you work at Amazon today, artificial intelligence is actually tracking—and rating—your productivity. Not only that, but you'll even get an automatic warning or termination if your performance is not meeting its standards, all without the intervention of a human.[20]

Likewise, Walmart is listening in on its employees through a special patented system to track certain performance metrics. It even listens for the sounds of rustling bags and scanners beeping in checkout lanes and eavesdropping to ensure employees are greeting guests.[21]

Domino's Pizza has developed a "Dom pizza checker" that combines sensor technology with AI and advanced machine learning that can be used to ensure each pizza is up to snuff; it alerts workers if they make an order wrong.[22] And all across America, there are now companies who employ individuals to track which websites their employees are browsing, even taking remote screenshots of workers' computers as evidence that they're doing personal work while on the clock.[23]

Is this ethical? Or is it just one more way for companies to monitor and improve employee performance? Actually, it's a very fine line. When it comes to privacy, most of us have been "sleepwalking towards a future without privacy" for some time, as one editor put it.[24]

Millennials, of course, have grown up in a connected society and are less concerned about their private data and online privacy than their parents ever were. Just look at the stream of public financial transactions between friends and acquaintances that appear in the feed on the popular mobile payment service, Venmo. Those apps on your iPhone are tracking your purchasing habits, political views, and sensitive personal data to sell to the highest bidder. The only generational difference here is perhaps the level of our alarm.

Privacy concerns aside, efficiency has always been the goal of automation. But what if the *ultimate* goal of artificial intelligence is to optimize humanity? It's already occurring in some industries. Call centers, for example, use AI software as a sort of adjunct to human managers with the goal of optimizing the performance of call center representatives.[25] The software monitors calls and even offers real-time feedback. Sounding sleepy? A coffee icon appears on the screen. Not empathetic enough? You'll see a heart icon.

Wired for Connectivity

As most of America shifted to working from home during the COVID-19 pandemic in spring 2020, it was modern technology platforms such as Zoom and Google Hangouts that kept remote teams communicating and collaborating. Personal cell phones, laptops, and internet service kept us each productive as our offices went dark.

In a surprising twist, many millennials said they missed the real-time interaction while other employees said they'd happily trade perks like the on-site gym at the office for their newfound creativity and productivity working from home. But either way, there's no question that the plethora of online tools and technology is what made it such a seamless transition for so many. As we've previously discussed, productivity actually *improved* for many reluctant employers who had predicted just the opposite.

Even The Sierra Group flexed during the pandemic to offering online training for adults with disabilities when stay-at-home orders went into effect. Instead of showing up in person for computer and business training, they logged on or participated by telephone if they didn't have an internet connection.

"Individuals with disabilities are already wired for adaptability. They live a daily life where adapting to change, flexibility, and creative teamwork are keystones to, well . . . living. This empowered our swift and seamless transition to remote learning at The Sierra Group Academy," explains Janet Fiore. "Attendance in classes was even higher during the 'stay at home order' because there were no transportation glitches or other disability-related obstacles to get in the way of full participation."[26]

Indeed, all this connectedness was already leading to less travel and more videoconferences, even before the pandemic. Seventy-five percent of senior execs said as much in one survey.[27] Plus, when it comes to "knowledge workers"—people whose jobs involve handling information—two out of five say they are interested in voice-activated virtual assistants[28] in lieu of humans to provide calendar updates, take notes during conversations, and transcribe voice prompts into email texts.

Is all this technology a good thing? That remains to be seen. One UK ergonomics company teamed up with a behavioral futurist to offer a stark warning of what the 2040 office worker may look like[29] if current tendencies go unchecked.

It comes in the form of "Emma," a life-sized doll with a bent back from too many hours hunched over a desk in a poorly designed workstation and varicose veins from poor blood flow due to too much sitting. "This level of associated health problems current workers face has not been seen since the Industrial Revolution," warns the company's CEO.[30] Back problems are mushrooming in younger and younger people as we spend our days staring down at our phones in a weight distribution never intended for the human head.

Replacing Humans?

One of the reasons that many of us may not end up bleary-eyed, with back problems in the way that that UK ergonomics company predicts is because we may be out of a job. Fifty-four million of us, in fact, over the next decade.[31] The biggest losers? Those of us who work as secretaries, administrative assistants, cashiers, and receptionists are at high risk of automation and job loss.

Look no further than the rapid pace at which grocery store chains have replaced human cashiers with self-checkout stations.[32] The COVID-19 pandemic only accelerated this trend in the rush to reduce customer-to-employee interactions and ensure social distancing. Labor-replacing automation is the new normal. It's happening to people who work in trucking, construction, carpentry, and grounds maintenance, too.

However, workers in education, social work, and health care are at low risk of being replaced by artificial intelligence. Supervisors, software developers, and CEOs are also more likely to retain their jobs.[33] Do you see a pattern here?

Occupations that include more discretionary decisions are less likely to be affected than those that do not. Post-secondary degrees frequently insulate against job loss in the face of automation. When you consider that black and Hispanic women are overrepresented in low-wage service jobs[34] with rote functions, you can begin to understand how AI is likely to have a negative and outsized impact on their lives, widening the existing socioeconomic divide that already exists in our country.

That's why digital literacy is more important than ever. Since 2000, most occupations in the US have required more of this skill set, although it varies from job to job. Digital proficiency is key to increasing earnings in an ever-more automated world.

There's no stopping the automation avalanche, though. *The robots are coming.* Just as the Industrial Revolution shifted work from farms to the factory with a sizeable downstream domino effect on families and American society, so too will there be a similar seismic shift due to artificial intelligence. Although the alarm on robots taking over the world has long been sounded, it's actually true now. The pace of automation is exponential today, not linear.

One Silicon Valley entrepreneur predicts that AI will affect the American workplace more dramatically than the internet has.[35] Sound far-fetched? In one study, authors estimated that nearly half of US jobs could be moved to computers over the next 20 years.[36] Why? Because when you pair the advance of machine learning with the availability of vast amounts of data, you can do a whole lot of things that only humans could do before. As computing speeds and data transfer ramp up along with advances in mobile technology, robots can even operate independently.

Let's consider a few examples:[37] for about $20,000, you can hire a robot called "Baxter" to dig a ditch, paint a house, lay pipes, or set bricks. No human required. Whenever there is a repetitive, physical task in a predictable environment, it's easy for a robot to excel. The Palm Beach County Court uses four robots now to read court filings, fill out docket sheets, and input data.[38]

The use of robots is also on the rise in grocery stores. "Marty," a slender, slow-moving robot with large eyes trolls grocery aisles, looking for spills and scanning hard-to-reach shelves to check on product availability. Giant Food Stores and other chains like it anticipate putting up to 500 Martys to work.[39] Heck, Marty can even find products for customers who don't speak English. When you consider that grocers and other retailers lose up to 4% of annual revenue due to out-of-stock or misplaced products alone, that's a major win.

Although jobs that involve managing people, social interaction, and creative thinking still require humans, plenty of other jobs typically reserved for human professionals are being outsourced to AI. For instance, a pharmaceutical company that used to outsource its financial forecasting to accounting students at Drexel University in Philadelphia has decided that computer algorithms are cheaper.

But honestly? No profession, job, or individual is *really* safe from automation. Just consider the achievements of IBM's Watson computer: "He" diagnoses cancer patients! By simply sifting through symptoms, medical histories, and cutting-edge research, he then suggests the most promising treatments.

In one head-to-head competition between AI and humans, JPMorgan Chase—one of the largest American banks—pitted human copywriters against an AI "message machine" for writing ads.[40] The result? The copy generated by the AI machine wrote ads that generated between two and five times the response of the human writer's copy, landing the software company a five-year contract for generating high-performing marketing creative.

All of this brings to mind the concept of "technological singularity." *Wikipedia* defines this concept as "a hypothetical point in time at which technological growth becomes uncontrollable and irreversible, resulting in unforeseeable changes to human civilization."[41] The basic idea here is that there is an explosion in intelligence with each iteration of improvement occurring faster and faster, leading to a "superintelligence" that is far greater than human intelligence. And that, according to believers, will signal the end of the human era!

Should We Pay a Guaranteed Income?

So, what should we do if vast numbers of Americans begin to lose their jobs to robots? After all, the coming shift to autonomous vehicles is just one example of dramatic changes automating the world of work. One study by researchers at Oxford University suggests that nearly half of all Americans are at high risk of losing their jobs to automation in the next 20 years.[42]

One idea is to pay workers a universal basic income (UBI). It's essentially a government stipend—almost a negative income tax—where workers without means receive a guaranteed payment. Sound crazy?

The idea is perhaps not as radical as it sounds. Proponents see it as a way to reform America's capitalistic system . . . to decouple work from income. Actually, Facebook's Mark Zuckerberg is a big fan of the idea. Even Andrew Yang championed a $1,000 monthly UBI for Americans (pre-pandemic) during his US presidential campaign. Proponents say it's the best way to end poverty.

As AI eliminates jobs, UBI could sustain workers and allow them to invest in retraining, skill development, and pursuit of new well-paid jobs. Artists—whose work isn't always valued economically—could be supported to do important work that society still values.

Around the world, governments have flirted with this concept. More than 130 countries have offered various types of conditional cash transfers to incentivize certain desired behaviors . . . where, say, someone gets a payment by sending their kids to school or for getting a health checkup.

Canada saw an 8.5% reduction in hospitalization and a decline in doctor visits in its UBI experiment in a Manitoba farming town. Finland experimented with the idea in 2017, giving the equivalent of $US635 per month to about 2,000 unemployed people for two years. It didn't help them get jobs but recipients did report feeling happier and less stressed as well as having more trust in other people and social institutions.[43]

In Stockton, California, there's a program called SEED—Stockton Economic Empowerment Demonstration—which experimented with universal basic income by offering 125 residents $500 per month for

18 months.[44] Beneficiaries say that that extra money offered the time to find meaningful work. When the COVID-19 pandemic hit in spring 2020, the mayor decided to extend benefits to more residents. Eleven other mayors took note, and at press time they were looking at implementing similar programs in their cities.

Even the state of Alaska currently gives each of its citizens an annual $1,000 to $2,000 check based on current oil prices. The money comes from the Alaska Permanent Fund, owned by the state and financed by oil revenues. Likewise, a casino on tribal land in North Carolina sends Native American Cherokee tribe members $4,000 to $6,000 per year.

And you know what? Economists who have studied the effect of these kinds of cash transfers say those tribe members don't work less. Actually, they enjoy better education and mental health with less addiction and crime, although that's not always been true during other state UBI experiments. Still, even in *those* cases, the slight reduction in work reported wasn't particularly compelling as a strike against UBI.

When the results were analyzed,[45] it wasn't clear people had dropped out of the labor pool forever. They weren't cutting back on hours. Some used the income to go back to school and to hold out for a better job while unemployed, rather than choosing just *any* job. And after all, that's perhaps a good thing. Employees with a good job fit are more likely to remain employed (higher retention reduces recruiting costs) and enjoy more personal well-being. Plus, it's hard to conclude much from those UBI programs many decades ago. They were generally short-lived and results not always well tracked.

Much more recently, the US government issued a flurry of stimulus checks during the COVID-19 pandemic, praying that a quick cash infusion might keep the economy from tanking. Meanwhile, European countries went about saving their economies in a more measured, consistent way.

In Amsterdam, for instance, the government covered 90% of out-of-work waitresses' wages. Denmark, the Netherlands, and the United Kingdom voted to "freeze their economies in place" by keeping at-home workers on their payrolls.[46] It's a great example of a policy designed for both the public and private good: workers are incentivized to stay home to stop the spread of the virus. They didn't have to worry about whether or not they could pay their bills, thereby heading to work when potentially symptomatic, infecting others.

The results on worldwide UBI experiments are mixed, but intriguing. Ultimately, though, I believe that there is dignity in work and most recognize that. As I noted at the outset, one of the very first questions we ask a new acquaintance is what they do for a living. It's a core part of our identity.

Human beings derive self-worth from both what they do and the productivity that feeds their families. Shouldn't we give them that opportunity through retraining when jobs become obsolete?

Socially Responsible Automation

It's time for employers to flex for the coming AI revolution *now*. As automation in many industries becomes the new normal, how will your organization respond?

Will you view it as a shortcut to cost cutting, profitability, and greater shareholder value? Or will you aim for socially responsible automation, when you recognize that the way you approach business goals through automation will have a ripple effect—for better or for worse—throughout your community?

Has your organization adopted digital accessibility standards? To avoid losing out on talent and customers, be sure that all websites, apps, and electronic documents are digitally accessible for everyone.

In 2016, Domino's Pizza found itself embroiled in a potentially expensive lawsuit after Guillermo Robles, a sight-impaired man, complained that he couldn't order a pizza online.

Robles's alleged was that he couldn't use his screen reader on the company's website, thereby impeding his access to goods and services that the pizza franchise, as a place of public accommodation, offered. And that is arguably a violation of the Americans with Disabilities Act. When the Court of Appeals in California sided with Robles, Domino's appealed to the US Supreme Court, which declined to hear the case, instead returning it to the lower court to determine if the website was really inaccessible. Although some courts are still split on the issue, it is becoming increasingly clear that websites *are* public accommodations and must be made accessible to all.[47]

You'll want to ensure your policies as well as your web presence are current to ensure ADA compliance. Are your organization's job announcements and online application systems accessible to persons with disabilities? One of the best ways to ensure all of that occurs is to invest in training for recruitment and procurement personnel as well as information technology professionals so they consistently include such features.

Are job interview locations physically accessible? When was the last time you reviewed your employment application form and employee handbook? Or rewrote job descriptions from an inclusion perspective?

Companies that are successful and creative at flexing with AI put people at the center of their decisions: both their customers and their employees. They adhere to their brand values during the transition in order to maintain their reputation as an employer of choice. They see themselves as more than the next product; rather, they're stewards of innovation and connected to their communities.[48]

They also commit to transparency by helping potentially laid-off workers connect with new opportunities, either within their organizations or elsewhere. Plus, when it comes to the best way to manage displaced workers due to the surge in artificial intelligence specifically, the answer lies in retraining, as I suggested previously.

We've always retrained Americans in the face of innovation. Just as men who once drove horses for buggies later learned how to assemble automobiles in factories, so too can we teach workers to excel in the age of AI. Help your employees prepare for the future by arming them with the skills they need to succeed in this brave, new, automated world.

At a minimum, you'll want to plan for the safety of your employees who will be working with robots. Be sure they also understand their role. If they'll be managing automated equipment, have you established an inspection protocol? Do they understand how to spot abnormalities in automated equipment to prevent breakdown? Consider, too, how employees and robots will move around a workspace together to avoid injuries.

Think big as you begin to sketch out the possibilities for AI in your organization. What might your employees achieve if they had machines to help? As Thomas Davenport, an MIT research fellow, suggests,[49] "Instead of seeing work as a zero-sum game with machines taking an ever-greater share, we might see growing possibilities for employment. We could reframe the threat of automation as an opportunity for augmentation."

In his *Harvard Business Review* article,[50] Davenport and his coauthor suggest five paths toward employability in an automated world. For example, can someone *step up* into a management role to add value by tracking the big picture? Maybe it's time to get that advanced degree. Or, perhaps employees can *step aside* by adding value alongside the robot. Imagine a writer or artist, for example, who offers multiple intelligences that can augment the output of a machine without intuition.

Other kinds of workers could *step in*—for example, a pricing expert who understands routine software decisions and can monitor outputs for optimization. By *stepping narrowly*, specialists might be able to contribute in a narrow niche for which AI doesn't yet exist. Also, employees—digital innovators, for instance—could *step forward* by building next-gen AI applications.

Will anyone be watching out for all of these workers attempting to discard outdated jobs and step into new ones? That remains to be seen. All of this automation is, frankly, making labor unions more uncomfortable than they already are about declining membership and their continued relevancy.

The United Food and Commercial Workers Union (UFCW) is watching the rise in automation closely to see how it affects workers. Marriott's unionized employees also went on strike in 2019 to protest the creep of automation and technology that continues to replace employees' jobs.[51] These days, their standard union contract typically requires advance notification about new technology and the ways it might affect jobs.

Labor's Next Frontier

The labor unions of today have a unique opportunity. Previously, we discussed the rise of organized labor as a major disruptor when America's postwar industrial economy matured. Yesterday's labor movement brought standardized hours, significant safety, and other protections to workers through collective bargaining.

But in recent years, as I mention in Chapter 2, organized labor has become less relevant; it's become *disrupted*. In a sense, it's become a victim of its own success. Due to its failure to evolve with the times, companies began to develop their own internal resources to help manage the concerns of workers. Internal personnel units grew into sophisticated and robust human resources and employee relations departments. Today, there's even a distinct course of study in American colleges for students interested in becoming human resources professionals.

Meanwhile, membership in unions is lower than it's ever been. Today's workers just don't buy the value proposition. Plus, unions just aren't keeping current with the changing trends in the world of work. For instance, they face stiff competition from digital platforms that offer workers similar kinds of assistance. One example: fruit pickers, who used to look for seasonal jobs on their own, now organize in online peer communities. That's given rise to an Australian website—fruitpickingjobs.au—that helps fruit pickers get visas, accommodations, and find jobs.[52]

If organized labor can flex by rising to the challenge to work with and not against employers to better advocate for workers disrupted by the wave of automation coming to America today, maybe, just maybe, it will have a new moment.

Perhaps, unions could once again become *disruptors*.

Recently, AFL-CIO Secretary-Treasurer Liz Shuler acknowledged as much in an interview on the AI revolution. She said, "It's going to be the next frontier for the labor movement. We can be the center of gravity for working people as they transition to new and better jobs, and make sure that they're getting the relevant training and services and voice that they need as the future of work is upon us."[53]

In fact, the AFL-CIO and member unions are working on a blueprint for responding to automation with "policy guardrails," as Schuler describes it. She sees the union's role as a kind of hub for best practices—a "platinum standard" for collective bargaining language that can be shared. The AFL-CIO is staking out a role as a vocal advocate of workers in industry partnerships and government committees.

In the end, none of us can stop the train of automation from remaking America; for better or worse, it's full speed ahead. Just as other disruptive forces throughout American history have brought new challenges and great benefits, so too will AI change the landscape of business forever.

The real question is: Will *you* be ready to flex as it remakes your organization?

Key Learning Points

1. The applications of artificial intelligence in America today are growing exponentially, transforming the world of work as dramatically as the Industrial Revolution once did in postwar America.

2. AI is improving our health, removing barriers for Americans with disabilities, connecting seniors, and even replacing humans in jobs that require repetitive, physical tasks. It's also tracking our movements, behavior, and personal data to understand our purchasing patterns, assess our productivity at work, and provide digital feedback to optimize performance.

3. Driverless vehicles are here. They're revolutionizing the transportation industry, which is changing supply chains, too.

4. Nearly half of Americans are at high risk of losing their jobs to automation in the next 20 years. Some suggest that paying unemployed workers a universal basic income

is the best way to avert poverty. But, although countries around the world—and even some states in the US—have earned some intriguing results with UBI experiments, the most promising way to adapt to the new world of AI is by retraining workers.

5. Companies that can effectively *flex* during the advance of AI will retool policies, protocols, and training now for socially responsible automation.

6 The Education We Need Is Changing

The progress of the world depends almost entirely upon education.

Source: George Eastman

E ven as artificial intelligence remakes nearly every American industry, the gap continues to widen between the skills workers need and the training they're getting (and paying for) at America's institutions of higher education.

Colleges, quick to raise tuition, are increasingly graduating students who aren't qualified for available jobs and that's a travesty. For an earlier generation, a four-year college degree was widely considered the passport to a satisfying career with upward mobility and a comfortable salary. It was what most parents wished for their children. Graduate education was the icing on the cake . . . a way to specialize further and cement earning power. But those outmoded ideas just don't match up to reality today. Today's college graduates frequently find themselves with dim job prospects and buried in debt acquired from costly student loans.

Earning power aside, there was a time that a liberal arts education was valued because it taught students how to be critical thinkers and to become well-rounded individuals well-versed in history, literature, and philosophy. Although those values are just as relevant in today's America, they fade into quaint fantasies when measured up against the practical reality of what education costs and what it can deliver for its exorbitant price tag. Universities aren't graduating students with marketable skills. In fact, there's a fundamental mismatch between what students are learning and how the world of work is changing.

Today, one out of four students who study at a nonprofit university—and one out of three who study at a public university— never even earn a degree.[1] The barriers to graduation seem insurmountable for many. Some students lack the support at school they need to overcome social and academic hurdles to succeed. Others could benefit from early intervention when the rigor of academics proves more than they anticipated.

But mostly, students who leave college without a degree just plain run out of money. Collectively, Americans owe more than $1.5 trillion in student loan debt.[2]

Let that sink in for a moment. What an incredible drag on the economy. As you've learned in our previous discussion about Gens X, Y, and Z, those new additions to the workforce won't be buying homes, having children, or otherwise making consumer contributions as they struggle to stay afloat.

Students used to be able to work summer jobs to offset costs during the school year. But today, tuition is so high that that's no longer possible. Plus, for those scrambling to pay, this often means not graduating on time, costing even more money. Or, students fold under the burden of working two jobs or caring for an elderly parent while attending school full-time.

It's no secret that a university education is unaffordable in America today. But what you may not realize is just how fast that cost has skyrocketed out of control. It's actually grown more than 74% between 2000 and 2016.[3] That's a shocking level of inflation.

Stratospheric costs are driving down enrollments at four-year academic institutions in particular, but that's not the only reason that fewer students are showing up. As I mention in Chapter 1, Americans are also having fewer children. Since the Great Recession in 2008, the birthrate has fallen by about 20%, equating to about 800,000 fewer births through 2018 and dropping fertility to its lowest level in 35 years.[4]

The COVID-19 pandemic is likely to accelerate this trend, with experts predicting up to 500,000 fewer births due to this influence alone. Just as fertility dropped 10% in the nine months during the 1918 influenza outbreak, stress and fear are not conducive to healthy pregnancies. Parents are exhausted working and caring for children at home and many are facing harsh economic realities due to sudden unemployment as they delay planned pregnancies.[5]

So fast-forward 18 years from now and you can start to see why college enrollments are declining. It's simple math . . . a declining population means declining college enrollments. In fact, experts predict a 20% decline by 2030[6]—and that was *before* the effect of lower births from the pandemic were factored in.

Meanwhile Jobs Sit Empty

Yes, you heard that right. Even as diligent college grads rack up interest on their loans at an alarming rate while tending bar and waiting tables in an attempt to skirt bankruptcy, employers struggle to attract workers with the skills they need.

One example: as industry flexes with automation courtesy of the AI revolution we've been discussing, employers are searching for workers who can manage machines, such as industrial engineers, for whom jobs grew 10% between 2012 and 2018.[7] Manufacturing industries have come a long way in their shift to technology and they need workers with the savvy and smarts to usher them into the future.

In fact, manufacturing in America is in the midst of a sea change. Just consider the shift at Chicago-based Pioneer Services, a company that today makes parts for Tesla. Two decades ago, employees needed uniforms to shield themselves from the abundant grease that spewed from outdated machines while making parts for heating and cooling systems. Today, the factory floor is full of t-shirt-clad coders with advanced degrees working on complex aerospace components.[8] More than 40% hold a college degree!

It's the same story at Advantage Convey in Raleigh, North Carolina. The company has invested $2 million over the past decade on machines to cut and bend metal for the conveyer belts it manufactures. As the industry shifted, workers who used to bend the parts by hand were reassigned or laid off in favor of hires who were more skilled employees. Today, Advantage only hires workers who have a minimum two-year degree. At Caterpillar, more than four in five jobs require or give preference to those with a college degree.

The Future of Education

As you can see, there's a critical misalignment here between students' rush toward a liberal arts college education and the excellent jobs available and waiting to be filled. Going to college because it "seems" like a good idea, without a plan or a university committed to learning outcomes that land a job, is risky business indeed.

The good news for college grads: increasingly, manufacturing companies are recruiting them for specialized jobs that require complex problem-solving skills. Regardless of whether the candidate has a liberal arts or a business degree, those graduates will be in demand. In the years to come, maybe those parents who value a college education will keep this top of mind as they steer Junior toward a college major.

Meanwhile, attendance at community college is on the rise. And there, the value proposition is far better. It's a win-win for both students and organizations because community colleges increasingly certify students for jobs that are ready and waiting.

Mira Costa College, for example, a community college in northern San Diego County, partners with a California phlebotomy training company to provide a series of four courses for certification (basic phlebotomy, advanced phlebotomy, applied phlebotomy, and an externship at a state-approved clinical lab or hospital).[9]

The national certifying exam is taken as part of the course with the promise that "accelerated training can get you into a job in just five months." Indeed, for community college students, who are just as anxious to land a great job as their peers at private four-year schools, these types of programs offer a solid path out of poverty, even without the ability to tap a wealthy, upwardly mobile alumni network.

And, it is much, much less expensive. Today, many community colleges even offer courses for rising high school graduates. My own niece, a recent graduate of a charter high school in Philadelphia, earned an associate degree from community college *while she was in high school*. Now she is headed to a private university to complete the final two years of her four-year university degree.

She can graduate in two years from that university *or* transfer into a specialized five-year program—such as nursing or occupational therapy—but finish by staying for just one additional year. Not only did she save two years of university tuition through this plan but also she saved two years of community college tuition. When my niece graduates, she (and her parents) will have significantly less debt than many of her peers.

My niece's decision to attend community college while in high school could be the factor that makes the difference in her ability to pursue—and fund—additional graduate education later. She would likely credit the charter school she attended for making this path possible.

Charter schools like hers are appreciated as a third option over public schools and more expensive private schools. Frequently, they offer smaller class sizes with more directed learning. Plus, they are also better at meeting the needs of students with individualized learning needs and those with developing interests—in science, engineering, or musical theater for a few examples—to dive deeper before settling on a career path in college. In short, there is less "teaching to the test."

Although charter schools help their students leapfrog their peers with an in-depth curriculum and community college enrollment, so too are community colleges advancing the career prospects of their students with the opportunity to develop real-world skills. Some are even creating "workforce development programs" by pairing courses such as project management and communication with technical training and actively partnering with organizations to recruit students.[10]

Mentorship, work-study programs, and formal internships are all bubbling up as creative, viable paths into the world of work. Plus, they offer a promising new channel for organizations to recruit more diverse students. These types of integrated school-work programs are particularly valuable because they level historic disparities for advancement between impoverished and wealthy students.

Employers have always preferred hiring new graduates with actual work experience in the field and that's meant a leg up for students who can afford to get free training in exchange for an unpaid summer internship subsidized by family. Those who need to pay rent through 40 hour weeks at Starbucks have lost out on such vital opportunities.

So academic partnerships in the world of work are welcome, indeed. Increasingly, community colleges are also partnering with local hospitals and health systems to graduate and recruit new nurses—LPNs and associate nursing degrees—in a shared commitment to a healthy community.

It's a particularly useful strategy for communities facing nursing shortages. Hospitals consult on the curriculum at the school and then offer internships to new grads. The trial internship period allows the prospective employee and the hospital to test out fit to ensure high retention.

Some public universities are also championing this approach to applied study. For example, Cal Poly Technic University, a nationally ranked school in San Luis Obispo on California's central coast has long enjoyed a reputation for meeting its "learn-by-doing" mission[11] as it graduates everyone from engineers to marketing managers and slots them into jobs. Nearly all students complete internships as part of their academic training.

Hands-on research and engagement in the community are at the core of every academic curriculum at Cal Poly. The result? A food science student graduates ready to start her own restaurant. A sorority student impaled by a stiletto at a party launches her own footwear business.[12]

Wait . . . *what?* Yes, indeed. When students spend their days continuously bridging academic theory and real-life experiences, creativity burns bright. After a lightbulb went on during the stiletto incident, she set to work learning how to negotiate a shoe contract and draft a provisional patent to manufacture sturdier shoes.

Another approach long since used but now even more popular at smart schools is an integrated approach to working and learning. For instance, Drexel University in Philadelphia and Northeastern University in Boston run co-op programs with businesses where students on a trimester schedule shift back and forth between trimesters learning and trimesters working in their field.

Not only do students learn how to apply what they're learning in the real world through hands-on experience but also they earn money while doing it, enabling them to pay down the cost of school. If they're fortunate, they'll also land a job with that company they worked for during school. This is a win-win-win!

And what about actual apprenticeships? In students' quest to improve ROI and avoid debt, more of them are choosing to pass on advanced degrees like MBAs—enrollment fell at such programs by one-third in two years recently[13]—in favor of applied specialized experience.

Would-be MBAs are moving to "start-up accelerator" programs instead. These three- to six-month programs provide enterprising self-starters with capital, mentorship, relationships, and the training they need to succeed.[14]

But there's no need for students to wait for postgraduate programs to get practical skills training in America today. Trade schools offer that from day one.

The Trade School Advantage

The reality is that vocational training reliably delivers when it comes to qualifying future workers for actual jobs. Trade schools go even further than community colleges when it comes to conferring specialized skills and training. They offer current hands-on training and, in some cases, even apprenticeships for electricians, painters, plumbers, and other construction and skilled trade careers.

But at today's trade schools, students can pursue a wide array of technical skills far beyond those traditional shop skills. Those options include subjects such as music production, filmmaking, and graphic design.

Personally, I've long joked that law school is really a very expensive trade school masquerading as postgraduate professional training. As you've just seen, trade schools today encompass far more industries than those formerly considered "blue collar." How is the analytical thinking required by law schools really so different from computer programmers who are learning logic? And besides, how many attorneys do you know who are actually capable of repairing the plumbing in their home?

A two-year trade school degree cuts college debt by half and leads to immediate skilled jobs. In 2018, the median salary for a chef and head cook was $48,460. For electricians, it was $55,190. Honestly, those are pretty close to the average salary for those with a bachelor's degree ($59,124) for the same year.[15] Plus, 40% of those who attend four-year universities drop out, as I've mentioned. (And those dropouts averaged just $38,376 in 2019.[16])

Previously, we talked about the number of high-paying manufacturing jobs sitting empty as machines replace people for repetitive tasks and companies seek out skilled managers. It's a compelling example of how education isn't keeping up with the skill sets employers need. In addition to the new job market driven by AI is the problem of all the available jobs sitting empty in the trades . . . jobs in carpentry, electrical, plumbing, and sheet metal work. According to the General Contractors of America, 70% of construction companies nationwide can't attract the workers they need.[17]

Business is booming in the trades and is expected to continue to expand in the years ahead. Even as the US government considers a much needed overhaul of US roads, bridges, rails, and airports,[18] the US Department of Education predicts a 68% shortage in workers over the next five years.

Many of these trade jobs don't require a bachelor's degree. But they sure pay well. Today, there are 30 million trade jobs with an average salary of $55,000 per year.[19]

But *those* are not the jobs kids are seeking.

And in large part, that's due to the expectations of their parents that they attend a four-year university. However, parents who look down on these opportunities for their children are actually rather short-sighted. They might consider that all is not lost if Junior does not head directly to university after graduating high school.

Instead of urging an ill-prepared student into a program that will not qualify her for a job after graduation, why not encourage her to start out in a trade school that *will* offer job opportunities? Or even encourage attendance at a vocational technical school while in high school?

If she's motivated and talented, she can always transfer to a four-year college later, maybe even convincing the company she works for to pick up the tab. A few years later, she could be embarking on specialized postgraduate education. Beginning a college career in trade school only has upsides for students who aren't ready for a four-year university at age 18.

In many European countries, the path toward trade school or university education diverges in high school. No one looks down on someone choosing a trade over an academic degree. It's all about finding the best *fit* for a student's passion and skills. When we consider the rapid pace of inflation in higher education and changing demographics here in the US, maybe we should be building more trade schools and fewer four-year universities.

Of course, just increasing access to trade schools won't solve the problem. We'll also need to work on parental attitudes so parents begin to appreciate the tremendous advantages and return on investment that vocational training can offer, as noted.

Trade schools are ever-evolving to equip students with practical skills that go far beyond just learning an industry. To deliver students truly prepared to enter the workforce of today, they'll also need to train students how to work remotely. In 2020, for example, 63% of organizations use a virtual workforce.[20] Plus, students will need to learn how to actually obtain one of those remote jobs.

With so many virtual teams, communication and collaboration skills will be essential, too. And then there's the skill of personal autonomy. Previously, we learned that traditional hierarchies are increasingly being abandoned in the American workplace in favor of flatter organizations where workers are adept at self-managing with leaders playing a supportive role. How will school train for that?

These are urgent topics for higher education to address now. But beyond our discussion of *what* must be learned to excel in the rapidly changing world of work still remains the question of *how* to pay for it.

Is Free Education the Answer?

As I mentioned previously in this chapter, the cost of education today is outpacing inflation dramatically. It's a runaway train. And that's a problem that is contributing mightily to the level of student debt, as we've been discussing. Finding a way to cut that cost in a meaningful way is central to the need for the reform of higher education.

One innovator, Mitch Daniels, former Republican governor of Indiana and now president of Purdue University in Lafayette, is doing his best to address and contain costs. In fact, he has frozen Purdue's tuition and fees at $9,992 for seven straight years, ever since he got the job. It's a significant achievement in the face of how education costs are climbing at other similar institutions.

Today, 60% of Purdue's grads leave without any debt. Compare that to the 70% of America's college students who take out loans and owe, on average, $25,000 when they leave. Holding the line on tuition at Purdue isn't just an incremental improvement in retooling for the future, as it might seem at first glance. Rather, it represents a new philosophy in education that differs starkly from other public universities. Daniels believes in *democratizing* college education . . . the idea that everyone should be able to afford school, whether they're wealthy or not.

Daniels has steadfastly resisted the impulses other colleges have succumbed to in their efforts to patch leaky revenue as enrollments have plummeted. He didn't drive up the percentage of out-of-state and international students to earn more revenue, for example. Although not without some controversy, the fact remains that Daniels did not hire a bunch of inexpensive adjunct faculty to replace full-time faculty; he sought out the best in their respective academic fields.

Despite his stubborn refusal to boost tuition to defray costs, the university earned an extra $100 million in higher enrollments from grateful students.[21] Purdue is adding research facilities, constructing new residence halls, and just added a learning center the size of a power plant.

Smart educational institutions are embracing creative ideas such as these. They understand the increasing skill gap their graduates face, the mountain of debt they're incurring, and the shift in demographics that will reduce their market for revenue from tuition.

They're also focused on how to support nontraditional students more effectively, improving the time to get a degree, graduation rates, and effective, personalized teaching for key learning outcomes. They're even becoming more entrepreneurial by investigating new revenue streams, such as contract research, continuing education, and intellectual property to compensate for a smaller tuition base.

But can't we do *more* than just hold the line on the current inflated cost of higher education? *Should* we make education free in the United States? Because that's how it works in plenty of other countries.

In Denmark, tuition is free; students just pay for books and living expenses. In practical terms, that means that every student can likely afford an education. Unlike in the United States, Danish students feel freer to pursue a passion at university rather than make a practical choice based on an economic calculus. In Germany, college students pay about $600 per semester, which is far more affordable than in the US. In Sweden, the government actually *pays* students $200 per month if they study full-time![22]

But make no mistake: European education systems also have their downsides. Germans are envious of the smaller professor-to-student ratios in the US. Swedes complain about graduating later than Americans. And Danes point out the problem with "eternity students," kids who find it so convenient to pursue one course of study after the next that they never get around to actually finding a job.

Isn't there a middle ground between "free" education and for-profit education? In some states, tuition is already free at community colleges. State schools also offer lower tuition. But can we be even bolder?

Mandatory Service Could Be a Game Changer

What if we could radically cut the cost of college education for today's students while also boosting volunteerism and eventually eradicating structural racism? That's the promise of mandatory service.

And it's sorely needed in America today. If America's civic health was an actual human patient, it would be on life support. Civic engagement is in freefall. Some 80 million voters didn't bother to cast a ballot in recent national elections[23] in a *democracy* that is founded on this very principle. Even as the latest scientific research points out that humans are actually hardwired to empathize and collaborate,[24] less than one-third of Americans say they belong to any group they feel is accountable and inclusive. That's a tragedy.

And this is where the idea of universal or mandatory service comes in. The idea of trading service for education actually has a long and noble tradition in the US. And it even exists today as the Reserve Officers' Training Corps (ROTC), a program that offers four years of paid college cost in exchange for military service.

Way back in 1944, in a bipartisan effort, the US Congress passed President Franklin Roosevelt's G.I. Bill of Rights to offer generous benefits to the country's WWII military members and veterans. It included low-cost mortgages for homes, low-interest loans to start businesses, one year of unemployment compensation, and it covered tuition and living expenses to attend high school, vocational school, or college. Wow!

More than 7.8 million vets used that bill to cash in on the American Dream. In fact, it is deemed wildly successful by most historians, who credit it, as much as anything, with strengthening the middle class. An important side note, however: a serious and unfortunate stain on that success record was the bill's unintended consequence of creating an even greater racial and economic divide between white and black America.

Although the bill didn't specifically exclude black vets, it also didn't enforce the extension of benefits to this group. Segregation in the South meant that universities refused to extend GI benefits to black veterans who had sacrificed for their country and who wanted to enroll, and that's where most of the black population lived so it was a widespread problem. Likewise, bankers denied these veterans home loans[25] due to simple discrimination (and as white Americans fled to the suburbs, black Americans languished in decaying inner cities). It's an American tragedy with an ugly legacy of disparity that still endures today.

In an attempt to spur civilian service, President Bill Clinton funded AmeriCorps, a voluntary civil service program in 1993. The idea is similar to the Peace Corps, established in 1961 by President John F. Kennedy. But, instead of sending volunteers around the world, AmeriCorps is dedicated to engaging participants in underserved communities right here at home in the US to meet urgent education, health care, and public safety needs.

Volunteers rebuild inner cities, care for the elderly, work on infrastructure projects, and teach in low-income areas. A smart mandatory service program would build on the strengths of AmeriCorps' pledge to engage America's volunteer spirit by requiring either military or civil service from every college-bound student. After all, American liberties come with personal responsibilities. Engagement is the mark of a true citizen.

How to increase volunteerism in America is the current focus of in-depth study by the National Commission on Military, National, and Public Service. And its work has been explicitly commissioned by the US Congress since 2017. In addition to reviewing the military selection process, the commission was tasked with offering recommendations to increase national and public service. The Commission says, "We envision a common expectation of service among the American people, so that no one is surprised by the questions 'How have you served?' or 'How will you serve?'"[26]

Furthermore, the commission recommended that Congress set up a $450 million fund for civic education and service learning. The goal: by 2031, all K–12 students receive in-class service experiences, one million 6th to 12th graders participate in a summer service program annually, and one million 9th to 12th graders participate in a semester of service each year.[27] Can you imagine? A bold vision indeed.

So, what if we took this idea one step further to *require* participation by every American in such a program? It's not much of a leap to amend the GI bill so that veterans of either civil service or military service can use benefits for education.

Opponents of mandatory national service say it's not needed . . . that we already have Teach for America, the Peace Corps, and AmeriCorps. Some don't like the idea of compulsory military service and prefer to maintain an army of volunteer professional soldiers (even though 30 countries, including Israel and even Switzerland, have found success with a mandatory service model).

Others say such a program would infringe on American freedoms, pointing out that the 13th Amendment to the constitution disallows "involuntary servitude." To that, I'd suggest that each of us has a shared obligation to contribute to our common good in the kind of "self-ruled society" that lies at the very heart of the American experiment.

Plus, there's an argument to be made that because Congress has the authority to provide for the country's common defense through conscription, so too can it require civil service. It's also worth noting that jurists have considered the involuntary servitude argument plenty over the years and come to the conclusion that mandatory service is within the zone of constitutionality and does not violate the 13th Amendment.[28] For example, federal judges have long since decided that national interests outweigh those of the individual when it comes to military service.

Although mandatory civic service is certainly distinct from military service, it also does not need to strip citizens of their civil rights and liberties in order for them to serve, as long as opportunities are well structured through reasonable assignments, work hours, and pay. Plus, we could include an opt-out option in the plan.

Those who don't wish to serve their country could opt out, as long as they understand they won't qualify for benefits such as Medicare, subsidized college loans, and mortgage guarantees. Those who feel mandatory service is government overreach would be free to make their own way, without any help from the Feds.

Still others are concerned that such a program would be just one more way for the rich to manipulate the system to exploit the less fortunate. Maybe a young athlete would lose valuable years to hone her talent. Or a struggling family would lose valuable childcare during a teenager's service. But is it really involuntary servitude if it's a *paid* position . . . much like the example of ROTC? There is no question that each of these arguments merit further consideration and discussion in a national dialogue.

But let's dream big for a moment. If America doesn't want to leave skilled jobs empty—even as the next generation of workers struggles to get a toehold in the world of work—isn't it time to explore a better way?

Why should the idea of mandatory service be any different than jury duty? It's generally accepted that jury service is a small price to pay to live in a free society. Mandatory national service embraces that same idea but goes even further, by offering valuable reciprocal benefits to those who serve.

Today, AmeriCorps actually offers an education award of $6,195 (as of 2019) to those who complete a term of service to pay education costs at qualified institutions or repay student loans, but that paltry amount won't be financing a four-year college degree anytime soon.

If the goal is to really lift Americans out of poverty who can't otherwise afford an education, we need a second GI bill that doesn't require potential students to mortgage their future. In today's political divide, it's hard to imagine overwhelming public support for a bill as generous as the original GI bill was, but I believe it could have a dramatic impact even if such a plan doesn't fully fund education. Imagine a tuition-sharing agreement, for example, in which students incur some of their tuition cost, but without the student loans that are accruing interest at a breakneck pace today.

It's also a cost-effective way to address urgent needs around the country. In fact, the Center for Benefit-Cost Studies in Education noted that current youth national service programs in the US cost $1.7 billion annually but bring in value of $6.5 billion . . . nearly four times their cost![29] Even the National Park Service saves 65% on maintenance costs annually by enlisting a volunteer conservation corps.

Plus, AmeriCorps members have helped 25,000 unemployed Kentucky coal workers find jobs in other industries. They cut violent crime in Detroit by 26% through neighborhood watches and escorting kids to school.[30] Just think about the tremendous impact of engaging all of America's youth in worthwhile projects like these.

What would the United States look like in 50 years if every inner-city kid spent a year helping a family in so-called flyover country bring in a harvest? How far could we come in unwinding and ending structural racism if kids from the heartland spent a year cleaning up a poverty-stricken inner-city neighborhood with no hope? Shared service can play an important role in knitting this country back together while addressing racism and reducing economic inequalities.

Just as exchange students in high school and college foreign exchange programs have long been emissaries abroad to bust myths and change stereotypes about their home countries, so too would America's young adults bring new perspectives, fresh ideas, and a well-nurtured volunteer ethic into their prime earning years to make a meaningful difference over a lifetime.

Mandatory service also offers the perfect antidote to the boomerang effect we're seeing today, where millennials are slow to settle on an academic major and career path, frequently moving back home with their parents and generally getting a slower start into the world of work. Instead, let's harness that energy and receptivity to new ideas by putting it to work in a year of service.

Ninety-seven percent of students who take a gap year today or spend a year studying abroad say the experience helped them mature. Why not seize this formative time and put it to good use with a structured opportunity?

In short, mandatory service is a great way to celebrate the diverse faces and talents of Americans today while breaking down barriers in race, class, geography, and income. As Gene Yaw, a Republican Pennsylvania state senator, once remarked, "We cannot generate enthusiasm for our way of life when less than 2% of our population has put forth any effort for our country."[31]

What Disruptors Will Do

In the face of all these changes to the world of work, some educational institutions are taking note, making changes, and reaping benefits.

True disruptors, like Southern New Hampshire University and Western Governors University, for example, are busy tapping into an underserved population: working adults who don't have time to commute to a traditional campus. These universities have flexed to online education with a focused curriculum that aligns to real jobs. And they're cutting costs while they do it by replacing college faculty with teaching assistants and "graders."[32]

Others are looking at ways to reinvent education in ways that align better to the current world. Imagine data-driven advising, for example, when students receive early alerts and reminders before things veer off track. It's an easy way to make a major difference in student success without costly in-person appointments.

Or think about those attorneys I mentioned who are studying law for three years in a vacuum in a version of a trade school. What if, instead, they moved to a model more like Drexel's co-op program? Aspiring attorneys could enroll in a two-year program that included a third year of actual time working in a law firm and perhaps a preceptorship in public service.

President Franklin Delano Roosevelt essentially did this, attending Columbia Law School for just two years before studying for and then passing the New York bar exam. And Abraham Lincoln never attended law school, which was not a requirement for sitting for the bar in the 19th century. What an applied way to learn about the profession.

Adapting higher education to better serve students also includes concepts such as block scheduling. There's no need for a defined academic calendar for college students. It's a relic left over from the days when students weren't available in summers because they were helping with the family harvest. And maybe the very idea of a physical campus that requires commuting is headed that way, too.

There's no good reason to let summer learning idle today or force students to meet in person for all courses. Universities nationwide jumped online quickly during the pandemic, proving that for many courses, online education is easy.

At a minimum, summer programs could bridge the academic year with activities such as peer tutoring, online tutorials, and peer-to-peer study groups. Block scheduling could also make a major difference for students working to balance job and family commitments with school.

What do all of these ideas share in common? They put the student's needs at the very center of the equation for success. It's not rocket science, but it's a novel approach for many of America's educational institutions.

Today, academic disruptors are going even further as they mull over the idea of "college by subscription." It works like this: students would just pay one monthly fee to access the course and advisers they're interested in. The Georgia Institute of Technology is considering just such a model, even expanding the offering to include access to worldwide mentors![33]

Smart schools are also taking advantage of AI computer simulations to advance learning in creative new ways. Look no further than Southern New Hampshire University's "Sandbox CoLABorative" for inspiration on what's coming. Its experts are reimagining the future of college education in a lab using everything from AI to computer simulations. The physical space in the lab is designed to inspire creativity, too. Teams can brainstorm during "free swim" in small on-site caves or huddle in restaurant-style booths.

Educators who flex are also taking note of the emerging gig economy. And that's great news: fully 89% of freelancers said they wished their school had better prepared them for the gig economy in a recent survey by the freelancer website UpWork.[34]

Babson College in Massachusetts hosts a course aptly titled "Entrepreneurship and the Gig Economy." What do MBA students learn?

How to get contract work, negotiate fees, and line up side hustles! Likewise, a communications professor at Wake Forest University in North Carolina teaches "Communication in Entrepreneurial Settings" where students learn about coworking, freelancing, telecommunicating, and even how to drive for Uber or host an Airbnb. Students learn how to evaluate potential gigs, too, by weighing the cost-benefit ratio. Even the career center at Wellesley, the prestigious and historic Massachusetts college, offers advice on how to get into the gig economy.[35]

How Well Is Your Organization Partnering?

If you own a business and are interested in recruiting the best and brightest, now is the time to identify and activate creative partnerships with local universities, community colleges, and other places students are congregating.

Go find them online! Massive online open classes—are convening students worldwide in academia and industry for collaborative learning in ways we never could have imagined just a few years ago.

Reach out to community colleges and local universities to propose a co-op program to train the workers *your* business needs.

Key Learning Points

1. University education in America today is unaffordable and isn't preparing students for available jobs. This is resulting in a fundamental misalignment between the way students are trained and the workers we need.

2. Meanwhile, community colleges are entering into creative partnerships with industry in a variety of industries to facilitate workforce development. Apprenticeships and trade schools are also filling these gaps.

3. Mandatory service could be a game changer as a solution that goes even further in absorbing tuition costs in exchange for volunteer service.

4. Disruptors in education are moving to online platforms, focused curriculums that align to real jobs, data-driven advising, block scheduling, and more. They're preparing students for the gig economy and AI revolution.

7 The Climate Is Changing

> It is not the strongest species that survives, nor the most intelligent.
> It is the one most adaptable to change.
>> Source: Charles Darwin, someone who knew a little something
>> about disruptors who *flex*

I f you're still wondering if climate change is real . . . or debating whether it's really caused by humans . . . or arguing that there has *always* been climate change . . . or dismissing calls for action on climate change as fear-mongering by liberals, you may not have all the information.

As an intergovernmental panel on climate change recently noted, "Scientific evidence for warming of the climate system is unequivocal."[1] Our world's climate is rapidly deteriorating and much of it is due to the impact of humans on our environment.

I do not profess to be a scientist; however, anyone who doubts this information has not examined the data. According to NASA, there is a 95% probability that climate change is a direct result of human activity since the mid-20th century.[2] Not only that, it's increasing at a rate that is unprecedented over many millennia. And this reality urgently requires a new set of skills to flex in the face of change.

As Andrew Winston, author of the book *The Big Pivot: Radically Practical Strategies for a Hotter, Scarcer, and More Open World*, explains: "Everyone is going to need to understand [climate change] the same ways you'd assume everyone in business needs to have some fluency in social media today, or that everyone would be able to use a computer 20 years ago."[3]

But before we examine the effects of climate change on business and the skills we will need to survive, let's back up and look more closely to understand what's actually occurring and how that's affecting life right now on the planet.

It's certainly true that there have been cycles of glacier advance and retreat for 650,000 years. But that all ended with the last ice age, which ushered in our modern climate and the advent of human civilization. Sure, the planet has experienced higher temperatures during other periods of history (such as during the Roman Empire[4]), but there's also no question that the dramatic climate change we are witnessing now is undeniably due to the huge impact of fossil fuels emitted by humans.

How do we know? Scientists use earth-orbiting satellites and other technology to collect and monitor climate data.[5] Much like glass in a greenhouse, the earth's atmosphere traps carbon dioxide, preventing it from escaping into space. And these greenhouse gases cause earth to warm in response. That causes global temperatures to rise, oceans to warm, ice sheets to shrink, causes glaciers to retreat, snow cover to decline, and sea levels to rise.[6] Oceans acidify and extreme weather events abound. No one on earth will be spared these devastating effects.

Clearly, the time to act is *now*. Not just to save our businesses, but to save our lives!

Here's a fact that may surprise you: interest and support for addressing climate change is growing rapidly by voters from *all* parties. For example, in a February 2020 survey sampling 1,991 registered voters, respondents said they are more concerned—48% more concerned—about climate change than they were a year earlier. By a margin of six to one, these voters want any national climate change solution to be bipartisan.

Fifty-eight percent of Republicans surveyed, said so, in fact. Plus, one in four American teenagers—the voters of tomorrow—have participated in a walkout, attended a rally, or written to a public official about their worry over global warming.[7] And that's good news because the US is by far the worst offender on the planet when it comes to emitting greenhouse gases.[8]

In light of these facts, it's a tragedy that climate change has become so viciously politicized in America today. On Earth Day 2020, Tom Ridge, the former governor of Pennsylvania, first director of homeland security in 2011—and my former boss—penned an op-ed in *The Atlantic* titled "My Fellow Conservatives Are Out of Touch on the Environment."[9] In the article, Ridge urged Americans to wake up to the crucial imperative of climate change and actively engage in solutions. His message wasn't new to me; he's been promoting governmental policies to reduce American dependence on fossil fuels ever since he was governor in the mid-1990s.

What surprises many is that as a Republican himself, he calls out conservatives specifically on their failure to widely recognize and respond to the threat of rising global temperatures. He also asks business leaders to assume personal responsibility for leading the change we need, precisely because the economic stakes for failure are so high.

We Are in a Death Spiral

If you were alarmed by the way the COVID-19 pandemic mercilessly ravaged the American economy, affected daily life, and stole most of the small pleasures you took for granted, consider that to be just a short preview of what's yet to come if we continue to fail to act on climate change.

Serious scientists and forecasters now project the earth to warm by at least 4°C (or 7.2°F) by the end of the century and possibly double that. In fact, a July 2020 study[10] suggests a 95% probability of doubling current carbon dioxide levels in the next 50 years to nearly reach that 4°C threshold. Much of the earth would become uninhabitable in such an event. And that's a serious problem. In fact, it *is* an existential threat.

Within the next 5 to 15 years, we can anticipate more heatwaves, food supply shortages, species extinction, violent storms, and rampant flooding. But that's just the beginning.

Here in the US, the Northeast could see new health risks from contaminated flood waters and the loss of iconic fisheries for Atlantic cod, sea scallops, and lobster. Plus, the annual cost of coastal storm surges across the Eastern Seaboard and Gulf of Mexico are expected to increase by $2 billion to $3.5 billion.[11]

The Southeast will see a boom in cases of West Nile Virus due to heatwaves. The Midwest will skyrocket in premature deaths due to an increase in ground-level ozone, even as pests increase and crop yields are diminished.[12]

Farmers in the Midwest and South will need to adapt in significant ways. Otherwise, they could experience at least a 10% drop in yields for crops such as corn, wheat, soy, and cotton; there's a 1-in-20 chance those losses could be greater than 20%.[13]

The Southwest will be ablaze with even more devastating wildfires than we've already seen, skyrocketing insurance rates for businesses and consumers alike. Deadly heatwaves in California led to rolling black-outs in summer 2020 as unprecedented demand for energy outstripped supply from the power grid.[14]

The rising sea level on the Pacific coast will erode two-thirds of beaches in Southern California. And, the chronic flooding of low-lying Hawaiian islands will displace more than 20,000 residents, even as it creates massive water shortages due to drought.[15]

In the Northwest, Alaskan fisheries will be devastated. In fact, Alaska is warming faster than any other state in the US. As greenhouse gas emissions raise the temperature in this region, the declining snowpack will increase wildfire risk there, too.

As greenhouse gases drive up temperatures, the US will need to construct the equivalent of 200 coal- or natural gas–fired power plants to keep up with new energy demands. And that will cost residential and business consumers about $12 billion per year.[16]

The US Will Face New Pandemics

Back in 2017, well before the world economy ground to a halt in the grip of the 2020 COVID-19 pandemic, Michelle De Pass, dean of the Milano School of International Affairs, Management, and Urban Policy at the New School in New York, offered some thoughts that now seem prescient. She warned: "We might . . . hear all about Ebola and other things, and not quite grasp that we are very, very vulnerable to [these kinds of epidemics] here in the United States, as well, because of what's happening with climate."[17]

Indeed, mosquito-borne illnesses such as malaria, Zika, and Dengue fever are particularly susceptible to extreme weather events due to climate change. Indian researchers have studied the link between malaria epidemics and excessive monsoons that breed those mosquitos extensively.[18] One analysis shows that malaria epidemics increase by fivefold after an El Niño event.[19]

Remember the Zika epidemic a few years back? In a perfect storm of disaster, a virulent new pathogen was introduced to South America, where the population had never before been exposed, just as the continent experienced an El Niño event (which causes excessive warming of surface waters in the Pacific Ocean). The resulting shifts in temperature and rainfall resulted in a massive increase in mosquitos.

But Zika, malaria, and Dengue are not American diseases, right? Unfortunately, as we've recently experienced firsthand, such outbreaks are not confined to third-world countries; they can and will wreak havoc on American shores too as our climate changes.

The transmission of COVID-19 from a bat to a human host in spring 2020 wasn't some random event never to be repeated again. As the human species relentlessly moves into lands formerly inhabited by wild animals, we destroy their habitat and squeeze them onto our very doorsteps. The transmission of runaway viruses is a predictable outcome of that reality.[20]

If we've learned anything from COVID-19, it should be to plan ahead for the next disaster now and do all we can to minimize dramatic shifts in climate change that make conditions ripe for devastation.

The cost to American lives, indeed all of life, is just too high to be complacent.

Squeezing the Bottom Line

Aside from the terrible toll that climate change will exact on humans as a species, and indeed all species, there's also an immediate and immeasurable threat to worldwide business as usual. For one thing, the dramatically changing weather patterns go straight to the bottom line. In one decade-long study comparing high snowfall years to low snowfall years between 1999 and 2009, researchers noted an economic impact of $173 million to ski resorts during years with low snowfall. That affects the numbers of skiers who visit, destabilizing resorts that depend on crowds.

Even before the pandemic closed down American workplaces, extreme weather events around the world have disrupted supply lines. Look no further than the recent experiences of Coca-Cola and Nike, both US corporate giants. Coca-Cola lost a 2004 operating license in India due to water shortages there.[21]

Plus, droughts and biblical-type floods disrupted the company's vital pipeline of sugar cane, beets, and citrus fruit required for production. Floods and droughts in cotton-producing regions of Thailand also disrupted Nike's supply chain for its cotton athletic clothes. Shortages, of course, lead to higher prices and more market volatility, which is never good for business.

As a result, both companies have flexed in the face of these climate realities. Coca-Cola is switching to new water conservation technology. Nike is using more synthetic material. But both companies are also lobbying governments around the world for more environmentally friendly policies.[22]

Climate Change Will Reshape the Workforce

As the changing climate alters our physical landscape, it will redistribute our workforce, too. And because we live in a global age, what happens across the ocean will send tremors across the sea to America.

Climate change is poised to shift the global labor landscape. For instance, the civil engineers who are responsible for planning and building our cities aren't prepared to deal with monster inundations of rain for six months followed by six months of drought that are quite likely to become the new normal.

And it's not just engineers, architects, or urban planners in at-risk cities who will need new skill sets to help us adapt. It's everyone from financial planners to farmers. Droughts and hurricanes on one side of the world, for example, will spike insurance premiums on the other.[23]

Just as sophisticated tech skills are sought by employers today, some believe employers will seek climate change competencies tomorrow. Smart organizations are planning ahead. Although the labor market for civil engineers appears to be playing catch-up, the energy industry has already begun to take the necessary steps to build a workforce for the future.

The evidence? In the first quarter of 2014, 32% of all energy industry jobs posted in the UK on Indeed.com were in the renewable energy sector. Three years later? Positions in this sector shot up to 51.5% of all energy industry postings.[24]

Money Talks

As you can see, climate change is a clear threat to business. Supply lines are threatened. The workforce isn't prepared. Brands are at risk. And that's because their customers increasingly care about how the products they buy and use impact on the environment.

According to one PR agency, more than 87% of US consumers make purchase decisions based on whether a company's social beliefs align with their own. Moreover, 75% of millennials say they would take a pay cut to work for a socially and environmentally responsible company.[25] And that's good news for the climate because it drives change in corporate behavior.

The other thing that's driving a change in corporate behavior with respect to climate is changing behavior by investors. In fact, today, many of them—including mutual funds and brokerage firms—use environmental, social, and governance (ESG) criteria to screen companies for socially conscious investors. ESG criteria look at how a company is treating its employers, suppliers, customers, and the community in which it operates. They also may include a company's energy use, pollution, commitment to conserving natural resources, and treatment of animals.[26]

Fortunately, large corporations are increasingly choosing to exercise their influence with both the government and markets to make their concerns about climate change known. In 2019, Goldman Sachs set a $750 billion target for funding green projects through loans, underwriting, advisory services, and investments. Goldman Sachs CEO David Solomon cited the "powerful business and investing case" for his decision to fund projects on renewable energy and sustainable transportation.[27]

It's Time to Get Busy

As a recent national report[28] on the economic risks of climate change in the United States points out, the cost of inaction on lowering greenhouse gases today increases the risk for tomorrow. In the same way that interest-only loans become prohibitively expensive over time, so too is climate change much like nature's own interest-only loan. Future generations will struggle to pay off that accrued interest on greenhouse emission, making it nearly impossible to pay down "emissions principal" for meaningful gains.

There's still time to enact meaningful change, but only if we get busy now through the use of a meaningful partnership between the federal government and the business community. That's why Tom Ridge has been so insistent that business leaders take action on climate now. In that 2020 Earth Day op-ed that I referenced previously, Ridge points out that the Republican Party, particularly, has abdicated responsibility on environmental issues, even though there is a growing chorus of concern from voters.

When I worked for him during his tenure as governor, I watched him put the ideas he espouses into practice with great success. I watched him eliminate red tape for businesses in Pennsylvania's Department of Environmental Protection while also holding companies accountable with appropriate oversight. Ridge's land recycling program remains a national model for cleaning and reusing contaminated parcels.

As governor, he established a voluntary partnership to reduce greenhouse gases, worked to ensure that the international Kyoto Treaty included reductions in greenhouse gases by all countries, cleaned up polluted industrial sites, and supported a revolving loan fund for clean water. He also allowed industries to take ownership, audit themselves, and then clean up those polluted sites without immediate government intervention. In short, Ridge offered a free market approach through partnership with state government that was not driven by overt government intervention.

In fact, under his leadership, the Commonwealth of Pennsylvania made a $650 million investment in a program called "Growing Greener," the state's largest ever investment to address environmental issues. Funding has only increased over time to clean up abandoned mines, restore watersheds, fund new parks and trails, and address thorny land use issues.

As Ridge points out, that program was proposed by a Republican governor and passed by a Republican-controlled legislature. Today, Ridge advocates for the Pennsylvania Conservative Energy Forum, a group working to increase support from conservatives for wind and solar energy solutions. Climate change isn't a liberal problem; it's everyone's problem.

A Carbon Tax Could Make All the Difference

A few pages back I shared with you the overwhelming support in America today for addressing climate change. You know what else Americans support? Charging fossil fuel companies for their carbon emissions (66% of respondents).[29] It's an idea that's not as radical as it might seem at first glance.

Such a policy puts a fee on fossil fuels such as coal, oil, and gas. The fee would start low, but grow over time and, as a result, drive down carbon pollution as both companies and consumers are incentivized to move toward cleaner, cheaper fuels.

Then, the money that's collected from this carbon tax could be allocated back to the American people—or to low-income Americans—who will bear a larger burden of climate change—to spend as they see fit. Because program fees would be paid from the taxes that are collected, the entire program would be revenue neutral. In other words, the government would spend nothing to fund it, nor would it earn money from the program.

This is the concept proposed by the Citizens Climate Lobby (CCL), a nonpartisan, nonprofit grassroots advocacy organization dedicated to enacting effective national policies to curb the climate crisis. For more than a decade, CCL has been training volunteer citizens to work with their congressional representatives to garner support for its carbon fee and dividend program. As a result, it's at the heart of several powerful bills pending in Congress.

And it could really work. Numerous studies have shown that cigarette taxes were directly responsible for dramatically curbing smoking among American youth. They found there was a clear and direct inverse relationship between the increase in the cigarette tax and the incidence of smoking between 1991 and 2017.[30]

A carbon tax is likely to have a similar effect on greenhouse gases; there's a strong consensus among economists that this is true.[31] They see a federal policy as the most cost-effective and least disruptive approach to making a real difference at the scale and speed that is necessary by spreading costs across the entire economy.

They say that such a policy will reduce America's emissions by at least 40% in the first 12 years if adopted and create 2.1 million new jobs with economic growth across America. How so? Consider the state of New Jersey, which recently announced its plan to build a 200-acre wind port for $300 to $400 million dollars. The project, which will provide infrastructure for offshore wind projects along the entire East Coast, is expected to create up to 1,500 jobs, not to mention hundreds of construction jobs in the state.[32]

Another aspect of CCL's legislative solution: imported goods would be assessed a border carbon adjustment and goods exported from the US receive a refund. Isn't that essentially a tariff, you might be wondering? In a sense, yes. However, this surcharge would only apply to goods imported from countries that do not have a similar carbon price. The carbon border fee adjustment makes up the difference.

That protects U.S. manufacturers and jobs. In short, a national carbon fee and dividend policy would be effective, good for Americans, and good for the US economy.

How do American companies feel about such a proposal? Again, you may be surprised. When President Donald Trump announced his plan in June 2017 to withdraw the United States from the Paris Accord—an international treaty signed by 195 countries committed to reducing greenhouse gasses worldwide—more than a dozen Fortune 500 corporate giants signaled their displeasure in a letter to the president.

From Apple and Google to BP and PG&E, companies pointed out that "U.S. business interests are best served by a stable and practical framework facilitating an effective and balanced global response."[33] Wall Street titan Goldman Sachs expressed outrage and Tesla's Elon Musk resigned in protest from the president's advisory board.

Randy Salim, who works with CCL's business outreach division, explains, "Of course businesses are concerned about their bottom line. But they also understand that the scientific evidence is in and that doing nothing is not an option. Climate change is here and the economic costs they will bear will only increase. Plus, it's important to remember that businesses are also run by humans who have children. They feel a moral responsibility to be part of the solution. Many want to be good corporate citizens who leave a resource rich planet to future generations."[34]

Many organizations are in favor of some version of a federal carbon tax and dividend plan such as the one proposed by CCL. It would drive behavior change with urgency while also putting money in the pockets of consumers (which increases GDP). Ultimately, a global price on carbon could create a standard price and policy across all markets. When all businesses in an industry equally shoulder the burden for the true costs of activities that increase greenhouse gases, the competitive playing field is leveled.

In one study[35] about the impact of carbon taxes on individual companies, researchers actually examined the effects of CCL's proposal on four leading information technology businesses in Silicon Valley using a $15 tax per $MTCO_2e$ (metric tons of carbon dioxide equivalent) as well as another proposal starting at $40 per $MTCO_2e$.

The takeaways? Both proposals would have insignificant to small cost impacts on all four businesses. In fact, the cost averaged 0.02% of operating expenses for three of four companies[36] . . . not even noticeable if it were passed on to consumers. Moreover, these large companies appreciated the idea of leveling the playing field because smaller competitors typically avoided these costs while they invested in renewable energy. Some also identified new commercial sales opportunities by branding their existing (or new) products as ecofriendly.

Such a plan offers a fair market–driven solution that would likely be more favorable to business than the more far-ranging "Green New Deal" resolution introduced by Representative Alexandria Ocasio-Cortez (D-NY) and Senator Ed Markey (D-MA). That approach recommends the US transition to 100% renewable, zero-emission energy sources (including electric cars and high-speed rail) within 10 years.[37]

It also plans for state-sponsored jobs, addresses the impact on poor communities, increases the minimum wage, prevents monopolies, and calls for universal health care. Some see the plan as unworkable government overreach and overambitious; they worry that unrealistic goals in the plan might mean losing key constituencies needed to pass it while the clock continues to run out on climate change.

That's why many businesses favor CCL's more focused solution and are actively lobbying today in Washington, DC, on behalf of the proposal. Today, even oil companies want to see a federal price on carbon![38]

American Industry Flexes

Increasingly, American businesses are working simultaneously on two fronts: advocating on behalf of federal action and working to reduce their carbon footprint within their industry.

For example, back in 2017, more than 75 organizations traveled to Washington, DC, with Ceres, a nonprofit that works with influential companies to tackle big environmental challenges. Those companies represented a combined market value of $2.5 trillion, employing more than 1 million US workers.[39]

Likewise, the Silicon Valley Leadership Group—the leading trade group for tech companies—actively lobbies on behalf of a national carbon fee and dividend program. They note that a federal policy on carbon pricing would have an impact across the economy more than 20 times greater than anything they could accomplish internally. They're asking for the federal government to engage as an active partner to bolster their organization-wide commitment.

In the meantime, the Silicon Valley Leadership Group has urged its members to shift to renewable energy for all data centers and commit to lowering their carbon footprint. Companies such as Capital One, Johnson & Johnson, Nike, and Unilever have committed to sourcing 100% of their electricity from renewable sources.[40]

The Sustainable Food Policy Alliance, a group with heavy-hitter members such as Mars and Nestle, is focused on driving public policies that "shape what people eat and how it impacts their health, communities, and the planet."[41] Cutting greenhouse gas emissions is one focus of the group, which favors a carbon pricing plan as well as regenerative agriculture practices and policy.

Regenerative agriculture practices and policies are on the rise. For example, member wineries of International Wineries for Climate Action, a fledgling group of eight international wineries launched in 2019, is dedicated to adopting a science-based approach to calculating and measuring the industry's greenhouse gas effect, identifying hot spots and then proactively taking steps to mitigate that effect through the adoption of regenerative practices.[42]

The group has an aggressive climate neutrality goal: to reduce emissions by 50% by 2030 and up to 80% by 2045. Why such an aggressive goal? Because it's in alignment with what global scientists say is necessary to avoid the worst effects of climate change.

One member of the group—Jackson Family Wines, with wineries in California and Oregon as well as worldwide—has been focused for more than a decade on its 2030 resiliency plan that encompasses all facets of its business by setting goals for social impact, land use, water, and emissions. Its goal is to become a climate-positive company by 2050, where the business actually repairs more than it emits.[43]

What About Smaller Businesses?

Clearly, large corporations have the resources to retool. But how would smaller businesses fare under a carbon-offset program? They too would be incentivized to rethink their impact. Transport companies would increasingly flex to hybrid or electric models, as we've discussed in Chapter 5 with the rise of electric trucks.

Manufacturers and shipping services might choose to adjust the weight of items and packaging. Because the true cost of materials would likely increase under such a program due to their carbon footprint, organizations could transition to materials that use renewable energy. Or, they might choose to pass on these additional costs to consumers if no good alternatives can be substituted for existing materials.[44]

The Free Rider Problem

Ultimately, the global community can only be successful combatting climate change if there are no free riders, countries that opt out of international agreements to hold emissions to an agreed-on level for the common good. It's just not fair for major emitters such as the US, India, and China to refuse to curtail greenhouse gases for political or any other reasons. Free riders continue to benefit from collective action without contributing themselves. That's why CCL's border fee adjustment is so powerful. It essentially *protects* trade competitiveness so that polluters don't enjoy an unfair pricing advantage.

One idea for formalizing this approach to combat the free rider problem is to incentivize participation through the creation of a climate club, the brainchild of William Nordhaus, a Yale economist.

Under Nordhaus's plan, member countries would put a price on carbon domestically while also sanctioning non-member countries. Countries could only join the club if they first addressed the true cost of using fossil fuels in their own economies . . . with, for example, a carbon tax such as the one we've discussed.

In any case, it seems clear that without a strong national policy for clean energy investments—one that stabilizes the economic impact of climate change on business and distributes those costs equitably—nothing we do as individual citizens or businesses can make a meaningful difference.

There's still time to avoid that doubling of carbon dioxide that scientists are predicting, but just barely. A national climate policy is our best hope to avoid disaster. And, recently, we've caught a glimpse of what bold action could still achieve.

When most of the world went into lockdown during the COVID-19 pandemic in spring 2020, people largely stopped driving their cars. And globetrotting in airplanes. That meant that 2.6 billion metric tons of CO_2—about 8% of the estimate for 2020—were never emitted into the atmosphere.[45]

As emissions dropped steeply, the planet responded quickly and dramatically. Small towns thick with pollution could suddenly see the Himalayas for the first time. National parks were flooded with wildlife reclaiming acres of habitat formerly ceded to humans. Geoscientists even recorded a reduction in seismic noise—the hum of vibrations in earth's core—as everyone just stayed indoors.[46]

Since then, many urban cities have begun to reimagine a new future, trading city centers jammed with cars for airy avenues dedicated to foot and bicycle traffic. Tourist-thronged cities—such as Venice, Italy—are rethinking the balance between desirable tourist dollars and better quality of life for residents.

America Must Flex

As Leaders, *you must make your views known*. Contact your congressional representatives. Let them know climate change is a top priority and share information about the ways it is adversely affecting your business.

By supporting congressional representatives that support action on climate change—both with your vote and your campaign contributions—you send a message that matters. Does your organization belong to a trade organization taking action on climate change? Frequently, such groups are concerned about climate issues but aren't actively funding legislators taking action. By reaching out and making your views known, you can help trade groups make a difference through concerted advocacy.

However, big challenges require bold commitments. Climate change is perhaps the most shocking and transformative of all the disruptive forces we've examined together in these pages. To meet this moment as a nation—to reverse our standing as the world's number-one polluter—it's going to take more than a call to Congress.

In short, it may also be time to reexamine America's addiction to car culture. Way back in 1953, in the Federal Aid Highway Act, President Dwight D. Eisenhower authorized a $27 billion infusion of funds into America's interstate highway system. At the time, he said our unity as a nation depended on individual and commercial movement through interconnected highways.

But today, our unity and prosperity as a nation depends on just the opposite: a shared commitment to saving the planet by reducing our carbon footprint. The automobile—which once stood as a symbol of American prosperity and freedom—has left us today with an illusion of independence as we idle for long hours snarled in traffic during our daily commute.

The way out? A national investment in reliable and efficient train travel. Why should Americans be any different from Europeans and Asians whose infrastructures are explicitly designed to efficiently move large groups of people with high-speed rail? In France, you can leave Paris after a full day of meetings and be sipping an aperitif on your terrace just 2.5 hours later. That train ride cuts four hours from the same journey by car!

So why is it that people who live in Philadelphia can't get to Boston in under seven hours? Or those who live in Los Angeles must drive eight hours to San Francisco? When Congress discusses major spending on infrastructure bills to fix America's roads and bridges, why isn't train travel also up for discussion?

From my office in downtown Philadelphia, I have a view of Philly's famed 30th Street train station and also a view of the Southeastern Pennsylvania Transportation Authority (SEPTA) trains. I'm reminded daily as I watch trains coming and going that it's quite easy to move around the region by train. Isn't it time for America to build on these successes?

It's worth noting that to truly create an effective high-speed rail system, our existing infrastructure would need to be significantly revamped. For example, because our nation is designed for cars, trains move across roads rather than using tracks that are raised over or run under roadways as they are in other countries. That requires trains to slow, losing precious travel time.

Back in 2010, President Barack Obama signed a $787 billion stimulus package, the American Recovery and Reinvestment Act, that laid out a vision for a world-class high-speed rail system with $10.1 billion allocated to this purpose. "There's no reason why Europe or China should have the fastest trains, when we can build them right here in America," he said at the time.[47]

Ultimately, most of those projects fizzled. In three states, Democratic governors who were awarded projects lost elections to Republicans who axed those projects. Other projects were underfunded. California's high-speed rail project—dubbed the "train to nowhere" by critics—hit no end of roadblocks between engineering problems, lawsuits, and an ever-expanding budget.

But President Obama had the right idea. America shouldn't give up on this vision. Other countries are doubling down on their commitment to moving large groups of people efficiently by train. In Europe, for example, citizens are choosing to forgo cheap puddle-jumper flights by EasyJet and Ryanair in favor of overland travel by train and ferry. They want to reduce their carbon footprint . . . to take personal responsibility for saving the planet.

Amtrak subsidies in the US could fast-track access to regional bullet trains. And our young adults can build next-gen travel through the mandatory national service plan we discussed previously.

Throughout history, Americans—and American businesses—have always demonstrated our ability to flex to realize a bold vision. From putting a person on the moon to rescuing Europe from Hitler, America's can-do spirit has been respected around the globe.

Now is the moment for each of us to actively engage in the battle to save our planet. American business can lead the way. There's never been more at stake.

Remember, as the young climate activist Greta Thunberg has pointed out, "The eyes of future generations are upon you."

Key Learning Points

1. Climate change is real and urgent. Not only is there ample scientific evidence to demonstrate the climate is changing quickly but also it's undeniably due to fossil fuels emitted by humans. Support for addressing climate change in the US is growing rapidly among constituents in all political parties.

2. Not only does climate change threaten our survival as a species but also it's squeezing the bottom line right *now* in a wide range of industries. Extreme weather events are disrupting supply chains.

3. A carbon tax could make all the difference. A federal policy that places a fee on fossils fuels would drive down carbon pollution in the same way that a cigarette tax successfully disincentivized smoking.

4. Disruptors are taking the lead on climate change by retooling, rethinking their impact, reducing their carbon footprint, and assessing key competencies future workers will need today.

5. Bold change requires bold ideas. A national commitment to investing in infrastructure for efficient train travel could improve quality of life while matching the commitment of countries worldwide to reduce emissions in a meaningful way.

CONCLUSION: WELCOME TO THE NEW AMERICAN CAPITALISM

Life is about learning … not just earning.
> Source: Michael O'Malley, History professor,
> George Mason University. © 2020.

N ow that you've gained an appreciation for how fast the world of work is flexing in the face of rapid change and the forces shaping that change, I'd like to leave you with an example of just what this new American capitalism looks like in practice when it's working very, very well.

In the end, as my boyhood friend, Michael O'Malley, often said to me over the years, life is indeed about learning and not just earning. The exciting news is that today—for those who flex—both things are possible. Furthermore, the market rewards organizations that are responsive to change, connected to their communities, and embrace learning.

Success in business today looks a lot more like a zig-zag than a straight line. And someone who understands that is Nick Bayer, founder and CEO of Saxbys, a coffee company with 23 cafes—and two more on the way—in the Philadelphia area.

At least . . . it probably *looks* like a coffee company to the casual observer or guest. But as Nick likes to say, Saxbys is a*n education* business fueled by *coffee*. He sees himself in the people business first and foremost. And he credits his phenomenal success to that thinking. It may not surprise you to learn that Saxbys' mission is to Make Life Better.

Saxbys has made *Inc Magazine's* list of 5,000 fastest-growing American companies for the last five years running. In 2019, the company unveiled its own coffee roastery by investing more than $1 million in state-of-the-art technology and bringing on a team with more than 50 years of experience in the coffee business to develop it. In summer 2020—in the wake of the COVID-19 pandemic—Saxbys flexed by moving online. Its e-commerce program grew by 1400%.

But as Nick sees it, none of those achievements really define success as a company. "When I was coming out of college, my professors were focused only on how to make money . . . what we call shareholder primacy today," he explains. "But that's not what I wanted to do. Sure, I wanted to run a successful for-profit business, but I also wanted to make a real difference in peoples' lives while I was doing it. I know that the more lives I change, the more successful Saxbys will be."

The Back Story

Nick Bayer grew up in Chicago with two teenage parents who never got a shot at a college education. Although his dad hoped to teach and coach, he couldn't without a degree. Eventually, he made a good living, but he missed his calling. And that's why they wanted so much more for Nick.

On the advice of his eighth-grade teacher, Mrs. Eischen, Nick's parents sent him to a private school on the other side of Chicago, where he then earned an athletic scholarship to Cornell University in Ithaca, New York. There, he made use of internships around the country and the contacts that go with them.

But when he was still in search of a calling closer to graduation, he reached out to Mrs. Eischen, his favorite mentor, to ask her advice. What did she say? "Make a difference. That's why I got into teaching." Nick heard the pride in her voice and recommitted to finding a calling that would give him that feeling.

So he looked around for a business that he could make profitable and use as a vehicle for good. "My greatest skill . . . the thing that makes my heart race . . . is doing good for other people," he explains. "I wanted a very people-centric business with little barrier to entry." And that's how he decided on coffee.

One of the things Nick loves about the coffee business is that it's a great equalizer. Saxbys serves more than 15,000 guests daily who are both millionaires and individuals sleeping on the street. Everyone enjoys a cup of coffee in the very same space. Everyone receives the same dignity and respect in this shared experience.

In the same way, Saxbys employs people whom it has hired out of homelessness as well as people with PhDs and MBAs. They all start at the same level with the same opportunity to grow. If you're disciplined, detail-oriented, outgoing, and exhibit a genuine love of doing good things for other people, you're likely a fit at Saxbys, wherever you sleep at night.

Double Impact

Nick Bayer has built a blockbuster company on his commitment to Make Life Better through a company that rises above the competition in one of the most competitive industries in the world. And he proudly measures that success by Saxbys' impending certification as a B Corp. Certified B Corporations are "businesses that meet the highest standards of verified social and environmental performance, public transparency, and legal accountability to balance profit and purpose."[1]

B Corps are companies dedicated to using business as a force for good. They are dedicated to reducing inequality and poverty, making the environment healthier, strengthening communities, and creating quality jobs with dignity and purpose.[2] The B Corp certification process is incredibly rigorous. In fact, it takes more than a year for auditors to assess an organization's impact to see if they qualify. (Just 1% of American companies do.)

So that's how Bayer defines his success at Saxbys. And that's the reason he's able to consistently recruit incredible talent with very little effort. "It's not that I've got a great sales pitch," he notes. "It's because it's easy to see how passionate everyone who works here is. When you work for a company you truly believe in, you're more productive and efficient than when you're just punching the clock."

And that shows in Saxbys' low employee turnover. Even though its café workers are primarily young students or those who are new to the workforce—a population most companies find hard to employ because of their propensity to jump to a next job (as we've discussed)—turnover at Saxbys is less than half the competition. Those youngsters are proud to be working for an impactful company and are looking to move up rather than leave.

Investing in Tomorrow's Leaders

In its quest for impact, Saxbys also began a partnership five years ago with Philly-based Drexel University to create an experiential learning platform for students. You may remember Drexel from our Chapter 6 discussion of first movers in education who are driving creative co-op programs.

Nick originally reached out to Drexel president John Fry after thinking back to his Cornell days when he served as an entrepreneur-in-residence. He remembered the Cornell Hotel School where students operated the hotel as part of their curriculum. He reflected on the valuable on-the-job training that students receive there and wondered: Could a similar concept work with students through a university partnership?

Fry was enthusiastic about the idea, so the two of them decided to convert a two-bedroom apartment just off campus into the first student-run café. Naysayers said student employees wouldn't be reliable. But they were wrong.

And that was the beginning of Saxbys' student CEO concept. From the outside, it may look like the undergraduates who run these cafes ("café executive officers," in Saxbys parlance) are simply managing an on-campus coffeeshop. And it's definitely true that these cafes represent explosive growth for Saxby as they open them across the region. Some of them serve 1,000 guests per day. In fact, by fall 2021, there will be 12 student-run Saxbys cafes that are affiliated with universities across Pennsylvania and Maryland.

But what these CEOs are really doing is learning how to lead an organization while they're still students. They lead a team of up to 70 of their student peers and manage a P&L statement as well as cost of goods sold and inventory. They make hiring, firing, and promotion decisions and are leading change in their communities through coordination with local clubs, university faculty, and other organizations.

A Saxbys student CEO earns the same full-time paycheck that non-student Saxby CEOs do while also earning full credit for the learning experience at Drexel. As you might anticipate, the gig is competitive. Students recognize the experience is not really about learning coffee, but rather about gaining the critical thinking and rigorous leadership skills that will land them a quality job in whatever industry *they* are pursuing.

In fact, one Drexel nursing student—recognizing that her early career experiences were likely to be more along the lines of paper pushing then bedside patient care—cashed in on her six-month Saxbys CEO experience by landing a top-tier nursing opportunity at the Children's Hospital of Philadelphia. It's perhaps the most competitive nursing co-op in the city. And it was her Saxbys' leadership experience that got her the job.

Flex

Saxbys also knows how to flex. When the COVID-19 pandemic hit . . . and then racial tensions boiled over . . . and then the economic crisis deepened, Nick Bayer doubled down on his mission. As his cafes shuttered—and the all-time high revenues in March flatlined—he spent five months holed up with a whiteboard thinking about disruption. He thought about companies that were disruptors and those who did the disrupting.

He asked himself and his team, "How are we unique? What are we truly great at? What do we want to be?" He reminded himself that through every economic downturn throughout history, there has been a corresponding uptick in enrollment in higher education.

He also pondered the widening gap between the cost of education and real wages even as universities continue to graduate students into the workforce who are mismatched with the job skills they need to succeed. "Wages have gone up just 11% in the last 25 years, not including inflation," he laments. "Even as the cost of higher ed has climbed 400%."

He thought about the relentless pace of technology and advances of machine learning and AI outsourcing jobs. And then he recommitted to his mission to Make Life Better.

Nick Bayer decided Saxbys was more important than ever. Why? Because Saxbys is about training power skills such as emotional intelligence, critical thinking, and cultural agility, the soft skills that machines can't match. Pre-COVID, Saxbys was a coffee company that did some work in education. But then Saxbys flexed and became an education company fueled by coffee.

In the same vein, Saxbys had always done work in diversity, equity, and inclusion (DEI). But instead of being an add-on to other work, as it had been, Saxbys flexed to make it core to its mission and training programs. In the same way that employees learn cash management or how to deescalate tense guest interactions, they now learn DEI.

In fact, the company's human resources team gets an additional 20 to 30 hours of DEI training annually for recruiting and talent development. And the corporate team—including every CEO—participates in DEI roundtables for candid conversations about hot topics. Because the roundtables are recognized as a safe space to ask tough questions and learn from people who know, they've earned 100% participation from employees.

When the Black Lives Matter movement mushroomed in the wake of the George Floyd killing in late spring 2020, Saxbys looked in the mirror and asked itself how it could best make a positive impact. The team then considered the upcoming month of June, historically recognized as Pride Month, where Saxbys had previously enjoyed a robust presence—and flexed. It centered its campaign around paying homage to the BIPOC (black, indigenous, people of color) gay individuals that started the PRIDE movement back in the 1980s and 1990s.

Saxbys celebrated and raised the voices of BIPOC trans individuals, interracial couples, and other BIPOC members of the LGBTQ community and focused on the idea of intersectionality by sparking conversations about the topic at its DEI roundtables. In short, Saxbys used the opportunity to highlight all of the ways all humans are interconnected despite race, class, gender, and sexual orientation.

It is leaders like Nick Bayer and companies like Saxbys who are the face of the new American capitalism.

This is the power of a company that can flex.

ABOUT THE AUTHOR

 RICK GRIMALDI is a partner at Fisher Phillips LLP, one of America's preeminent management side labor and employment law firms. Rick's unique perspective comes from his diverse career in high-ranking public service positions, as a human resources and labor relations professional for an international hi-tech company, and in private practice as a partner in a large law firm working with companies to help them adapt to the ever-changing business environment, achieve their workplace goals, and become better employers. Rick has been recognized as one of America's best lawyers in 3 of the last 4 years.

ACKNOWLEDGMENTS

First and foremost, I want to express my gratitude to my clients, past and present, many of whom have become friends and valued partners. I hope I have in some small way contributed as much to you as a trusted advisor as you have contributed to my growth and understanding of how you work every day to make your own organizations a better place for your workers, customers, and clients. You have made this 30-year project possible.

I also want to thank my colleagues and partners at FisherPhillips. I am honored to work with such dedicated and talented lawyers and professional staff who, in my opinion, are second to none in understanding the world of work and the need to continuously grow to better serve clients as true partners.

I am particularly grateful to Chris Stief, who was among a handful of individuals at the firm who were aware of this project and who embraced it from the start.

I also want to thank FisherPhillips managing partner, Roger Quillen, whose steady and steadfast leadership has guided our firm, not only through the COVID-19 international health crisis but also into a bright future of unlimited possibilities. I am incredibly appreciative of his support for this project.

Thank you to Luke McDaniels and Kelsey Beerer, who enthusiastically volunteered to assist me with research. They exemplify the talented and dedicated lawyers who are the future of the legal profession.

A special thank-you to Clare Block and Donna Kearney, two of the best marketing professionals in any industry. Clare was there at the beginning when I first pitched the project and provided me with great counsel on the daunting process of writing a book. Donna listened to me discuss the project and immediately had the vision to see its potential.

Thank you to David Maher, a brilliant young bio engineer on the front lines of the technology revolution, who read early chapters of the book and offered insight into the challenges faced by talented graduates entering the rapidly changing workforce of today.

I am forever grateful to my friend, Lisa Borin Ogden, for reading early drafts and providing suggestions on how to make this book better. Lisa is a gifted intellect and talented lawyer who understands the policy and political importance of creating a stronger American economy by embracing progressive ideas.

A special thank-you to cochair of the bipartisan House of Representatives Future of Work Caucus, Lisa Blunt Rochester, and her staff. Representative Blunt Rochester has dedicated her political and personal life to creating economic empowerment and equal opportunity for all. She understands the changing face of the American workplace and how we, as a nation, must work together and flex to meet that future. I am honored that she penned the foreword to this book.

Thank you to Tristan Higgins, professor Alexander Cocron of Johns Hopkins University, Janet Fiore, Nick Bayer, Raymond Smeriglio, and Randy Salim for sharing their stories of addressing, through their work, the challenges facing Americans of all stripes as the world around us shifts.

I am grateful to the contributions of my friend and former radio cohost, Dr. Anthony Mazzarelli. He is one of the smartest individuals

I know. As a physician, bioethicist, lawyer, author, co-president and CEO of Cooper University Health System, he is on the front lines of health care and recognizes that compassionate, forward-thinking health care delivery is critical to our future. He also encouraged me to write this book and provided valuable insight into the impact of health care on the American workplace.

I am incredibly grateful to the talented Chris Roman and Dottie DeHart, who worked with me throughout this project and who kept me on track and on deadline. A special thanks to Wiley Publishing along with Brian Neill, Deborah Schindlar, and Susan Geraghty for believing enough in a first-time author and the project to put it into print.

Thank you also to Lori Armstrong Halber, who is a tireless advocate for women and their value as leaders in the workforce and with whom, over the years, I discussed many of the ideas in this book.

I am very appreciative for the assistance of the Greater Philadelphia Chamber of Commerce and especially president and CEO Rob Wonderling, Tara Orio, Brook Leshak, and Tom Levy. Together, they work tirelessly to improve the economic, educational, and cultural soul of the greater Philadelphia region.

Thank you to my former boss, former Pennsylvania governor and our country's first Homeland Security secretary, Tom Ridge, a man with character and unwavering ethics, who saw long ago that environmental stewardship and business profitability is not a zero-sum game.

A special thank you to the management, past and present, of talk radio 1210 WPHT in Philadelphia for having the fortitude to put a radio neophyte on air, especially David Yadgaroff, Mike Baldini, Ed Palladino, and Jared Hart. Each mentored me in the world of talk radio. They showed me the value of using new and multiple media platforms to stay relevant.

Finally a very special thank you to my family, Lynn, Taylor, Paige, Madisen and Nate for believing that this book could get written and who could not have been more supportive as I worked on it while doing my "day job," and who patiently endured my rants during COVID.

NOTES

Chapter 1   The World Is Changing

1. Frey, William H. "The U.S. Will Become 'Minority White' in 2045, Census Projects." Brookings Institution. March 14, 2018. https://www .brookings.edu/blog/the-avenue/2018/03/14/the-us-will-become-minority-white-in-2045-census-projects/

2. Teare, Gené. "Study of Gender Diversity in Private Company Boardrooms." Crunchbase.com. December 11, 2019. https://news .crunchbase.com/news/2019-study-of-gender-diversity-in-private-company-boardrooms/

3. United States Census Bureau. "Older People Projected to Outnumber Children for First Time in U.S. History." March 13, 2018. https:// www.census.gov/newsroom/press-releases/2018/cb18-41-population-projections.html

4. Ibid.

5. Schaeffer, Katherine. "U.S. Has Changed in Key Ways in the Past Decade, from Tech Use to Demographics." Pew Research Center. December 20, 2019. https://www.pewresearch.org/fact-tank/2019/12/ 20/key-ways-us-changed-in-past-decade/

6. Centers for Disease Control National Center for Health Statistics. "Trends in Fertility and Mother's Age at First Birth Among Rural and Metropolitan Counties: United States, 2007–2017." National Vital Statistics System, 2007–2017. https://www.cdc.gov/nchs/data/ databriefs/db323_table-508.pdf#1

7. Grawe, Nathan. "Americans Are Having Fewer Kids. What Will That Mean for Higher Education?" *Harvard Business Review*. October 17, 2019. https://hbr.org/2019/10/americans-are-having-fewer-kids-what-will-that-mean-for-higher-education

8. Grawe, Nathan. "Demographic Changes Pose Challenges for Higher Education." Econofact.Org. July 29, 2018. https://econofact.org/demographic-changes-pose-challenges-for-higher-education

9. Fry, Richard, and Paul Taylor. "Hispanic High School Graduates Pass Whites in Rate of College Enrollment." Pew Research Center. May 9, 2013. https://www.pewresearch.org/hispanic/2013/05/09/hispanic-high-school-graduates-pass-whites-in-rate-of-college-enrollment/

10. Ibid.

11. Gross, Ashley, and John Marcus. "High-Paying Trade Jobs Sit Empty, While High School Grads Line Up for University." *All Things Considered*. NPR. April 25, 2018. https://www.npr.org/sections/ed/2018/04/25/605092520/high-paying-trade-jobs-sit-empty-while-high-school-grads-line-up-for-university

12. Erard, Michael. "How the English Language Has Evolved Like a Living Creature." *Science*. November 1, 2017. https://www.sciencemag.org/news/2017/11/how-english-language-has-evolved-living-creature

13. XPressPlanet. "7 Best Technological Inventions of 21st Century." June 30, 2017. http://xpressplanet.com/greatest-technological-inventions/

14. Stillman, Jessica. "Breakthrough Technologies That Are About to Change the World." *Inc*. Aril 25, 2017. https://www.inc.com/jessica-stillman/10-breakthrough-technologies-that-are-about-to-change-the-world.html

15. Kaufman, Ellie, Ross Levitt, Rene Marsh, and Gregory Wallace. "How Climate Change Will Impact the US." CNN. November 27, 2018. https://www.cnn.com/2018/11/27/health/climate-change-impact-by-region/index.html

16. Ibid.

17. Ibid.

18. Henriques, Martha. "Will Covid-19 Have a Lasting Impact on the Environment?" BBC. March 2020. https://www.bbc.com/future/article/20200326-covid-19-the-impact-of-coronavirus-on-the-environment

19. Scoble, Robert, and Shel Israel. *Age of Context: Mobile, Sensors, Data and the Future of Privacy* (Patrick Brewster Press, 2013).

Chapter 2   America Was Built on Change

1. "History of the Organization of Work." *Encyclopedia Britannica*. March 20, 2020. https://www.britannica.com/topic/history-of-work-organization-648000

2. "Economic Activity: Pre-Industrial, Industrial & Post-Industrial." Study.com. March 22, 2020. https://study.com/academy/lesson/economic-activity-pre-industrial-industrial-post-industrial.html

3. Ibid.

4. "History of the Organization of Work."

5. "1860 United States Census." *Wikipedia*. March 15, 2020. https://en.wikipedia.org/wiki/1860_United_States_Census

6. "Industrial Revolution." *Wikipedia*. March 15, 2020. https://en.wikipedia.org/wiki/Industrial_Revolution

7. "Division of Labour in the Workplace." *Encyclopaedia Britannica*. March 17, 2020. https://www.britannica.com/topic/history-of-work-organization-648000/Division-of-labour-in-the-workplace

8. Ibid.

9. "What Effect Did the Shift in Economic System (from a Largely Agrarian Society to an Industrial Society) Have on Workers and Their Family?" enotes. March 22, 2020. https://www.enotes.com/homework-help/effect-shift-economic-system-agarian-to-industrial-543319

10. "Assembly Line." *Encyclopaedia Britannica*. March 17, 2020. https://www.britannica.com/technology/assembly-line

11. Lewis, David L. *The Public Image of Henry Ford: An American Folk Hero and His Company* (Detroit: Wayne State University Press, 1976), 43.

12. US Diplomatic Mission to Germany. "Income Data for 1900 and 1910 (Assumes One Wage Earner per Household)." April 20, 2020. https://usa.usembassy.de/etexts/his/e_prices1.htm; "Ford Model T." *Wikipedia*. April 20, 2020. https://en.wikipedia.org/wiki/Ford_Model_T

13. Coase, R. H. "The Nature of the Firm." *Economica*. March 21, 2020. https://onlinelibrary.wiley.com/doi/full/10.1111/j.1468-0335.1937.tb00002.x

14. Alexander Cocron. Telephone conversation with the author. March 19, 2020.

15. Ford, H., and S. Crowther. *My Life and Work* (New York: Doubleday, Page & Co, 1922).

16. "Assembly Line."

17. "The Development of Industrial United States." National Museum of American History. March 25, 2020. https://americanhistory.si.edu/presidency/timeline/pres_era/3_657.html

18. "Labor Movement." History.com. March 26, 2020. https://www.history.com/topics/19th-century/labor#section_7

19. "National Labor Relations Act." National Labor Relations Board. March 27, 2020. https://www.nlrb.gov/guidance/key-reference-materials/national-labor-relations-act

20. Ibid.

21. "The Labor Movement and The Great Depression." History.com. March 27, 2020. https://www.history.com/topics/19th-century/labor#section_7

22. Mayer, G. *Union Membership Trends in the United States* (Washington, DC: Congressional Research Service, 2004).

23. "How the GI Bill's Promise Was Denied to a Million Black WWII Veterans." History.com. March 28, 2020. https://www.history.com/news/gi-bill-black-wwii-veterans-benefits

24. "American Women in World War II." *Wikipedia*. March 26, 2020. https://en.wikipedia.org/wiki/American_women_in_World_War_II

25. Ibid.

26. Mitra Toosi, "A Century of Change: The U.S. Labor Force, 1950–2050," *Monthly Labor Review* (May 2002), 18.

27. Ibid, 15.

28. "Jackie Robinson." *Wikipedia*. March 26, 2020. https://en.wikipedia.org/wiki/Jackie_Robinson

29. *Brown v. Board of Education,* 347 U.S. 483 (1954).

30. "Kodak." *Wikipedia*. March 26, 2020. https://en.wikipedia.org/wiki/Kodak

31. "Cellphone Cost Comparison Timeline." technology.org. September 18, 2017. https://www.technology.org/2017/09/18/cell-phone-cost-comparison-timeline/

32. "IPhone Beat Toilet in 'Greatest Inventions.'" techradar.com. March 27, 2020. https://www.techradar.com/news/phone-and-communications/mobile-phones/iphone-beats-toilet-in-greatest-inventions-list-690485

33. "How Has the Workplace Changed?" work.chron.com. March 27, 2020. https://work.chron.com/workplace-changed-12823.html

34. "Progressive Conservatism." *Wikipedia*. April 28, 2020. https://simple.wikipedia.org/wiki/Progressive_conservatism

35. "Progressive." Merriam-webster.com. March 28, 2020. https://www.merriam-webster.com/dictionary/progressive

36. "Following from the Front: The Future Management Model." Forbest.com. March 28, 2020. https://thefutureorganization.com/following-from-front-future-management-model/

Chapter 3   The People Who Work Are Changing

1. Schaeffer, Katherine. "U.S. Has Changed in Key Ways in the Past Decade, from Tech Use to Demographics." December 20, 2019. https://www.pewresearch.org/fact-tank/2019/12/20/key-ways-us-changed-in-past-decade/

2. "Spring Release Extends Reach & Engagement with Launch of Touchpoint and More." Vision Critical. April 15, 2020. https://www.visioncritical.com/blog

3. Schaeffer, "U.S. has Changed in Key Ways."

4. United State Census. "Older People Projected to Outnumber Children for First Time in U.S. History." March 13, 2018. https://www.census.gov/newsroom/press-releases/2018/cb18-41-population-projections.html

5. Chotiner, Isaac. "How Old Is Too Old to Work?" *The New Yorker*. March 8, 2020. https://www.newyorker.com/news/q-and-a/how-old-is-too-old-to-work

6. Hoffower, Hillary. "Millennials Only Hold 3% of Total US Wealth, and That's a Shockingly Small Sliver of What Baby Boomers Had at Their Age." BusinessInsider.com. December 5, 2019. https://www.businessinsider.com/millennials-less-wealth-net-worth-compared-to-boomers-2019-12#:~:text=Millennials%20only%20hold%203%25%20of,boomers%20had%20at%20their%20age&text=When%20boomers%20were%20roughly%20the,according%20to%20recent%20Fed%20data

7. "A Shift in Workplace Demographics: How Organizations Need to Adapt for the Aging Workforce." Jacob-Morgan podcast. April 18, 2020. https://thefutureorganization.com/workplace-demographics-organizations-aging-workforce/

8. "Companies Offering Returnship Programs." Glassdoor. July 9, 2019. https://www.glassdoor.com/blog/6-companies-offering-returnship-programs/

9. Bott, C. "Firms Can Do More to Help Attys Who Feel 'Always on Call.'" *Law 360*. Fisher Phillips. March 3, 2020. Portfolio Media.

10. Plante, S. "Inside FIRE, the Implausible Millennial Movement to Save, Invest, and Quit the American Workforce." Vox. March 18, 2020. https://www.vox.com/the-highlight/2020/3/18/21182018/financial-independence-retire-early-fire-early-retirement-mr-money-mustache-pete-adeney

11. "The New Plus-One: Babies in the Workplace." Fisher Phillips. March 18, 2020. https://www.vox.com/the-highlight/2020/3/18/21182018/financial-independence-retire-early-fire-early-retirement-mr-money-mustache-pete-adeney

12. "The 4-Day Workweek: Helpful Innovation or Expensive Risk?" Fisher Phillips. February 28, 2020. https://www.fisherphillips.com/resources-newsletters-article-the-4-day-workweek-helpful-innovation-or?click_source=sitepilot06!6061!cmdyaW1hbGRpQGZpc2hlcnBoaWxsaXBzLmNvbQ==

13. Hirsch, A. "Is Conversational Recruiting the Solution to Finding Millennial Talent?" Society for Human Resources Management. June 11, 2019. https://www.shrm.org/ResourcesAndTools/hr-topics/talent-acquisition/Pages/Conversational-Recruiting-The-Solution-to-Finding-Millennial-Talent.aspx?utm_source=Editorial%20Newsletters~NL%202019-6-11%20HR%20Daily&utm_medium=email&utm_campaign=HR%20Daily&mkt_tok=eyJpIjoiTmpZellUWTJPR1F6WmpkaiIsInQiOiJOTEk0dW9tQTFlQytTNk44eVVFbUM3OU5YRitJT1wvcXljZ0RlWEsyZzRKcFBFcjZBT2Y3KzVCQ2M2M2MlwvSE9KYnd2VnR1WGNHSTJ0bVkrclJuTjE1aUIrYUI3RXdENXBFTWVuNG1YdkNIK2JTbGZ3S3hVOEZtOEZJZzA1NXc3cFg5In0%3D

14. "Generation Z Says They Work the Hardest but Only When They Want to." Society for Human Resources Management. June 11, 2019. https://www.shrm.org/ResourcesAndTools/hr-topics/employee-relations/Pages/Gen-Z-worries-about-work-skills.aspx?utm_source=Editorial%20Newsletters~NL%202019-6-11%20HR%20Daily&utm_medium

=email&utm_campaign=HR%20Daily&mkt_tok=eyJpIjoiTmpZellU
WTJPR1F6WmpkaiIsInQiOiJOTEk0dW9tQTFlQytTNk44eVVFbU
M3OU5YRitJT1wvcXljZ0RlWEsyZzRKcFBFcjZBT2Y3KzVCQ2M2
MlwvSE9KYnd2VnR1WGNHSTJ0bVkrclJuTjE1aUIrYUI3RXdENX
BFTWVuNG1YdkNIK2JTbGZ3S3hVOEZtOEZJZzA1NXc3cFg5In
0%3D

15. Ibid.

16. Berger L. "The Rise of Women in Corporate Board Rooms."
     Forbes.com. February 13, 2019. https://www.forbes.com/sites/
     forbescoachescouncil/2019/02/13/the-rise-of-women-in-corporate-
     boardrooms/#db3a2084085e

17. U.S. Board of Labor and Statistics. "A Century of Change: The U.S.
     Labor Force, 1950–2050." May 2002. https://www.bls.gov/opub/mlr/
     2002/05/art2full.pdf

18. "New Report Says Women Will Soon Be Majority of College-Educated
     U.S. Workers." NPR. June 20, 2019. https://www.npr.org/2019/06/
     20/734408574/new-report-says-college-educated-women-will-soon-
     make-up-majority-of-u-s-labor-f

19. "Women Outnumber Men in Law School Classrooms for Third Year
     in a Row, but Statistics Don't Tell the Full Story." Jurist.org. March 5,
     2019. https://www.jurist.org/commentary/2019/03/pisarcik-women-
     outnumber-men-in-law-school/

20. Ayes, R. "Women Make Up a Majority of Essential U.S. Coronavirus
     Workers." Axios.com. December 5, 2019. https://www.businessinsider
     .com/millennials-less-wealth-net-worth-compared-to-boomers-2019-12
     #:~:text=Millennials%20only%20hold%203%25%20of,boomers%20
     had%20at%20their%20age&text=When%20boomers%20were%20
     roughly%20the,according%20to%20recent%20Fed%20data

21. Epperson, S., and M. Fox. "This Critical Link Could Help Bridge
     America's Racial Wealth Gap." CNBC. June 26, 2020. https://www
     .cnbc.com/2020/06/26/this-critical-link-could-help-bridge-americas-
     racial-wealth-gap.html

22. Walker, D. "Are You Willing to Give Up Your Privilege?" *New York Times*. June 25, 2020. https://www.nytimes.com/2020/06/25/opinion/black-lives-matter-corporations.html

23. Noland, M., and T. Moran. "Study: Firms with More Women in the C-Suite Are More Profitable." *Harvard Business Review*. February 8, 2016. https://hbr.org/2016/02/study-firms-with-more-women-in-the-c-suite-are-more-profitable

24. Ibid.

25. LaMagna, M. "Having More Women on Your Boards Can Boost Your Investment Returns." MarketWatch. March 8, 2018. https://www.marketwatch.com/story/something-amazing-happens-when-you-have-3-or-more-women-on-a-company-board-2018-03-08

26. "Women on Corporate Boards: Quick Take." Catalyst.org. May 27, 2020. https://www.catalyst.org/research/women-on-corporate-boards/

27. Nold and Moran. "Study."

28. Teare, G. "2019 Study of Gender Diversity in Private Company Boardrooms." Crunchbase.com. December 11, 2019. https://news.crunchbase.com/news/2019-study-of-gender-diversity-in-private-company-boardrooms/

29. *Regents of Univ. of California v. Bakke,* 438 U.S. 265 (1978).

30. Ibid. See also Gratz *v.* Bollinger, 539 U.S. ___, 123 S.Ct. 2411, 156 L.Ed. 2d 257 (2003).

31. Finley, T. "Four Key Points That Debunk Misconceptions Around Affirmative Action." HuffPost. August 3, 2017. https://www.huffpost.com/entry/affirmative-action-still-matters_n_5981d9b6e4b0353fbb33e1bb

32. Frey, W. "The U.S. Will Become 'Minority White' in 2045, Census Predicts." Brookings Institute. May 14, 2018. https://www.brookings.edu/blog/the-avenue/2018/03/14/the-us-will-become-minority-white-in-2045-census-projects/

33. United States Census. "Older People Projected to Outnumber Children for First Time in U.S. History." March 13, 2018. https://www.census.gov/newsroom/press-releases/2018/cb18-41-population-projections.html

34. Frey, "The U.S. Will Become 'Minority White' in 2045, Census Predicts."

35. Long, H., and A. Van Dam. "Most New Working-Age Hires in the U.S. Are People of Color." *The Washington Post*. September 9, 2019. https://www.washingtonpost.com/business/economy/for-the-first-time-ever-most-new-working-age-hires-in-the-us-are-people-of-color/2019/09/09/8edc48a2-bd10-11e9-b873-63ace636af08_story.html

36. "A Dozen Facts about Immigration." The Hamilton Project. April 24, 2020. https://www.hamiltonproject.org/papers/a_dozen_facts_about_immigration

37. Ibid.

38. Ibid.

39. Ibid.

40. Lorenzo, R., N. Voigt, M. Tsusak, M. Krentz, and K. Abouzahr. "How Diverse Leadership Teams Boost Innovation." BCG.com. January 23, 2018. https://www.bcg.com/en-us/publications/2018/how-diverse-leadership-teams-boost-innovation.aspx

41. "Surf the Next Wave in Workplace Accommodation." Fisher & Phillips LLP white paper. February 20, 2020.

42. "PWC18th Annual CEO Survey 2015: A Marketplace Without Boundaries? Responding to Disruption." January 2015. https://www.pwc.com/gx/en/ceo-survey/2015/assets/pwc-18th-annual-global-ceo-survey-jan-2015.pdf

43. Lindson, J. "Why Companies Who Hire People with Disabilities Outperformed Their Peers." *Fast Company Magazine*. March 13, 2019. https://www.fastcompany.com/90311742/why-companies-who-hire-people-with-disabilities-outperformed-their-peers

44. O'Connor, John M. "Why You Should Hire Someone with a Disability." *Forbes*. September 13, 2018. https://www.forbes.com/sites/forbescoachescouncil/2018/09/13/why-you-should-hire-someone-with-a-disability/#7476a73b1039

45. Tristan Higgins, telephone conversation with the author, April 8, 2020.

46. "The Value of Belonging at Work: New Frontiers for Inclusion." BetterUp. April 24, 2020. https://get.betterup.co/rs/600-WTC-654/images/BetterUp_BelongingReport_091019.pdf

47. Ibid.

Chapter 4   The Way We Work Is Changing

1. Grisham, G. "The Gig Economy Is Gaining Steam in Canada." Gig Employer Blog. Fisher-Phillips. December 20, 2019. https://www.fisherphillips.com/gig-employer/the-gig-economy-gaining-steam-in-canada

2. Raton, R. "Freelancing in the Age of Unicorns: Understanding the Role of the Gig Economy in the Modern Workforce." Fisher-Phillips. January 31, 2017. https://www.fisherphillips.com/resources-articles-freelancing-in-the-age-of-unicorns-understanding

3. Sherman E. "49% of Americans Under Age 35 Now Report Having a 'Side Hustle.'" *Fortune*. June 6, 2019. https://fortune.com/2019/06/06/gig-economy-part-time-jobs/

4. *The Gig Economy and Florida's Workforce System*. CareerSource Florida and Cambridge Systematics. May 11, 2020. https://careersourceflorida.com/wp-content/uploads/2019/12/Gig-Economy-Report.pdf

5. Davidson, P. "Unemployment Soars to 14.7%, Job Losses Reach 20.5 Million in April as Coronavirus Pandemic Spreads." *USA Today*. May 5, 2020. https://www.usatoday.com/story/money/2020/05/08/april-jobs-reports-20-5-m-become-unemployed-covid-19-spreads/3090664001/

6. Johnson, M. "Trends in the Modern Workplace: Is Your Business Up with the Times?" Instapage blog. May 8, 2020. https://instapage.com/blog/modern-workplace-trends

7. Jen Su, A. "Finding Balance as a Dual-Career Couple." *Harvard Business Review*. July 29, 2019. https://hbr.org/2019/07/finding-balance-as-a-dual-career-couple

8. Maurer, R. "SHRM: Employers Say Remote Work Not Here to Stay." Society for Human Resources Management. May 5, 2020. https://www.shrm.org/ResourcesAndTools/hr-topics/talent-acquisition/Pages/SHRM-COVID-Coronavirus-Employers-Say-Remote-Work-Not-Here-to-Stay.aspx

9. Naylor, B. "For These Federal Employees, Telework Means Productivity Is Up, Their Backlog Is Down." NPR. May 5, 2020. https://www.npr.org/2020/05/05/850106772/for-these-federal-employees-telework-means-productivity-is-up-their-backlog-is-d

10. "Study: Work-Life Balance in the Modern Workplace." Comparably.com. May 12, 2020. https://www.comparably.com/news/study-work-life-balance-in-the-modern-workplace/

11. Harrington, J. "Wouldn't You Like 30 Mandated Days Off? Here Are the Countries with the Most Vacation Days." *USA Today*. July 23, 2019. https://www.usatoday.com/story/money/2019/07/23/paid-time-off-countries-with-the-most-vacation-days-brazil-france/39702323/

12. "Study: Work-Life Balance in the Modern Workplace." Comparably.com. May 14, 2020. https://www.comparably.com/news/study-work-life-balance-in-the-modern-workplace/

13. Meneghello, R. "Misclassification Doomsday in California: State Supreme Court Adopts Notorious 'ABC' Test." Gig Employer Blog. Fisher-Phillips. May 1, 2018. https://www.fisherphillips.com/gig-employer/misclassification-doomsday-in-california-state-supreme-court

14. Wallender, A. "Uber's Worker Business Model May Harm Competition, Judge Says." Bloomberg Law. June 21, 2019. https://news.bloomberglaw.com/daily-labor-report/ubers-worker-business-model-may-harm-competition-judge-says

15. Ratton, R. "United States: Freelance in the Age of Unicorns: Understanding the Role of the Gig Economy in the Modern Workforce." Fisher-Phillips. January 31, 2017. https://www.fisherphillips.com/resources-articles-freelancing-in-the-age-of-unicorns-understanding

16. Hussain, S. "Freelance Journalists File Suit Alleging AB5 Is Unconstitutional." *Los Angeles Times*. December 17, 2019. https://www.latimes.com/business/story/2019-12-17/freelance-journalist-ab5-lawsuit

17. "Gig Economy Feels Bit of California Law in Uber, Lyft Ruling." Bloomberg Law. August 11, 2020. https://news.bloomberglaw.com/daily-labor-report/gig-economy-feels-bite-of-california-law-after-uber-lyft-loss

18. Meneghello, R. "Congress Debates What 'Future Of Work' Could Mean for Gig Economy." FisherPhillips. October 29, 2019. https://www.fisherphillips.com/gig-employer/congress-debates-what-future-of-work-could

19. Meneghello, R. "In Big Win for Gig Companies, California Voters Approve Proposition 22." Fisher Phillips. November 5, 2020. https://www.fisherphillips.com/gig-employer/big-win-gig-companies-california

20. Kim, T. "The Gig Economy Is Coming for Your Job." *New York Times*. January 10, 2020. https://www.nytimes.com/2020/01/10/opinion/sunday/gig-economy-unemployment-automation.html

21. "Blogging Statistics in 2020." Tech Jury. May 11, 2020. https://techjury.net/stats-about/blogging/

22. Wellington, E. "From Men's Style Pro Blogger to Shoe Designer, Sabir Peele Says Guys 'Are Having More Fun.'" *The Philadelphia Inquirer*. February 29, 2020. https://www.inquirer.com/columnists/mens-style-pro-sabir-peele-shoes-menswear-philadelphia-blogger-designer-20200229.html?utm_medium=referral&utm_source=ios&utm_campaign=app_ios_article&utm_content=XUZA3C5TKJENZDILCW6OZSGHCU

23. "Blogging Statistics in 2020." Tech Jury. May 12, 2020. https://techjury.net/stats-about/blogging/

24. "Kaiser Shipyards." *The Oregon Encyclopedia.* May 13, 2020. https://oregonencyclopedia.org/articles/kaiser_shipyards/

25. Packer, M. "Will Life and Medicine Go Back to Normal After COVID-19?" *MedPage Today.* April 20, 2020. https://www.medpage today.com/blogs/revolutionandrevelation/86211?fbclid=IwAR3kzVmn RflqcXsUZWdQT9bzdCyPf6ZXyruyJcwb839FMbIH5hO5F44kdWg

26. Livingston, S. "UnitedHealthcare Plans Bigger Presence on Obamacare Exchanges." Modern Healthcare. June 15, 2020. https://www .modernhealthcare.com/insurance/unitedhealthcare-plans-bigger-presence-obamacare-exchanges

27. "What's So Special About Finland?" *The Atlantic.* July 7, 2016. https://www.theatlantic.com/international/archive/2016/07/nordic-american-dream-partanen/489032/?fbclid=IwAR13Fgafb7AH2FTvt-TGPy__VV2jeJ5sT0JdalIytbPwH1sccpo7De3R_qc

28. "U.S. Health Care from a Global Perspective, 2019: Higher Spending, Worse Outcomes?" The Commonwealth Fund. January 30, 2020. https://www.commonwealthfund.org/publications/issue-briefs/2020/jan/us-health-care-global-perspective-2019

29. "How Does Health Spending in the U.S. Compare to Other Countries?" Peterson-KFF Health System Tracker. December 20, 2018. https://www.healthsystemtracker.org/chart-collection/health-spending-u-s-compare-countries/#item-start

30. Ibid.

31. Gawande, A. "The Cost Conundrum." *The New Yorker.* June 1, 2009. https://www.newyorker.com/magazine/2009/06/01/the-cost-conundrum

32. "New Interactive Map: Variations in Medicare Costs." Committee for a Responsible Federal Budget. June 27, 2013. https://www.crfb.org/blogs/new-interactive-map-variations-medicare-costs

33. Ibid.

34. "Coronavirus Drives Health Insurers Back to Obamacare." *Politico*. May 14, 2020. https://www.politico.com/news/2020/05/14/ coronavirus-health-insurers-obamacare-257099

35. Ferh, R., D. McDermott, and C. Cox. "Individual Insurance Market Performance in 2019." Kaiser Foundation. May 13, 2020. https://www .kff.org/private-insurance/issue-brief/individual-insurance-market- performance-in-2019/

36. Trzeciak, Stephen, and Anthony Mazzarelli. *Compassionomics: The Rev- olutionary Scientific Evidence That Caring Makes a Difference* (Pensacola, FL: Studer Group, 2019). Interview with the author. May 6, 2020.

37. Gawande, A. "Big Med." *The New Yorker*. August 6, 2012. https://www .newyorker.com/magazine/2012/08/13/big-med

38. Said, C. "AB5 Gig Law Enforced: California Sues Uber and Lyft to Make Drivers Employees." *San Francisco Chronicle*. May 5, 2020. https://www.sfchronicle.com/business/article/AB5-gig-law-enforced- California-sues-Uber-and-15248217.php

39. Grimaldi, R. "Philadelphia's Portable Benefits Plan Could Be Gig Economy Model." Fisher-Phillips. November 12, 2019. https://www .fisherphillips.com/gig-employer/philadelphias-portable-benefits-plan- could-be-gig

40. Grisham, G. "Gig Workers in New Jersey May Soon Have Benefits." Fisher-Phillips. March 3, 2020. https://www.fisherphillips.com/gig- employer/gig-workers-in-new-jersey-may-soon

41. Meneghello, R. "Seattle Creates Minimum Wage for Gig Econ- omy Drivers." Fisher-Phillips. November 27, 2019. https://www .fisherphillips.com/gig-employer/seattle-creates-minimum-wage-for- gig-economy

42. Maurer, R. "Getting the Most from the 'Alternate Workforce." Society for Human Resource Management. June 18, 2019. https://www .shrm.org/ResourcesAndTools/hr-topics/talent-acquisition/Pages/

Getting-the-Most-from-the-Alternative-Workforce.aspx?utm_sourceu=
Editorial%20Newsletters˜NL%202019-6-18%20HR%20Daily&utm
_medium=email&utm_campaign=HR%20Daily&mkt_tok=eyJpIjoi
TVdZMFpXVTFPV0psWldKaiIsInQiOiJqbStpeWtGZlZsaFJSRUhr
T3JmcUpwOGF3QlNhSE5tbU9LXC9qY1hpbHRtRtY0xzWHo5SzU4
N3Y2RzlyK245NktJYUI3MENpTFdNYXdmdGtIa3hqTlNHY1R2Y
UhvQWtOSG5ORDVOYUZNdXZQSElBbBUxRU01zSmJHaWozYlp
LdFlQR08ifQ%3D%3D

43. Ibid.

Chapter 5   The Tools of Work Are Changing

1. Interview with the author. May 26, 2020.

2. "7 Best Technological Inventions of 21st Century." XpressPlanet
   .com. June 30, 2017, http://xpressplanet.com/greatest-technological-
   inventions/

3. McKinnon, J. "Trump Seeks to Boost AI as Chinese Competition
   Grows." *The Wall Street Journal.* February 11, 2019. https://www.wsj
   .com/articles/trump-seeks-to-boost-ai-as-chinese-competition-grows-
   11549861260

4. "As IPO Soars, Can Uber and Lyft Survive Long Enough to Replace
   Their Drivers with Computers?" *The Washington Post.* March 29, 2019.
   https://www.washingtonpost.com/technology/2019/03/29/even-with-
   ipo-billions-can-uber-lyft-survive-long-enough-replace-their-drivers-
   with-machines/

5. Potts, J. "How Driverless Trucks Will Change Supply Change Strategy."
   Inbound Logistics. December 29, 2016. https://www.inboundlogistics
   .com/cms/article/how-driverless-trucks-will-change-supply-chain-
   strategy/

6. "Driverless Trucks Being Tested Right Now on Public Roads."
   CBSNews.com. March 3, 2013a. https://www.cbsnews.com/news/
   driverless-trucks-being-tested-on-public-roads-60-minutes-2020-03-
   13/

7. Ibid.

8. Ibid.

9. Ibid.

10. Lambert F. "Tesla Cybertruck: Elon Musk Scraps Plan to Make Electric Pickup Smaller." Electrek.com. May 23, 2020. https://electrek.co/2020/05/23/tesla-cybertruck-elon-musk-scraps-plans-smaller-electric-pickup/

11. Ibid.

12. "The Employment Impact of Autonomous Vehicles." US Department of Commerce. May 25, 2020. https://www.commerce.gov/sites/default/files/migrated/reports/Employment%20Impact%20Autonomous%20Vehicles_0.pdf

13. Ibid.

14. Hasani A. "A Transit Employer's Duty to Bargain over Automation: Introduction." Fisher-Phillips. September 16,, 2019. https://www.fisherphillips.com/autonomous-vehicles-blog/a-transit-employers-duty-to-bargain-over-intro

15. Del Ray, J. "How Robots Are Transforming Amazon Warehouse Jobs—For Better and Worse." Vox.com. December 11, 2019. https://www.vox.com/recode/2019/12/11/20982652/robots-amazon-warehouse-jobs-automation

16. Terdiman, D. "How AI Is Helping Amazon Become a Trillion Dollar Company." *Fast Company*. October 5,, 2018. https://www.fastcompany.com/90246028/how-ai-is-helping-amazon-become-a-trillion-dollar-company

17. "Global Recruiting Trends 2018." LinkedIn. January 9, 2018. https://app.box.com/s/y5i7635s15rx3yl78hj5jlnnh02asa75/file/263787765561

18. Harwell D. "A Face-Scanning Algorithm Increasingly Decides Whether You Deserve the Job." *The Washington Post*. November 6, 2019. https://www.washingtonpost.com/technology/2019/10/22/ai-hiring-face-

scanning-algorithm-increasingly-decides-whether-you-deserve-job/?
wpisrc=al_trending_now__alert-economy–alert-national&wpmk=1

19. Bogen, M. "All the Ways Hiring Algorithms Can Introduce Bias." *Harvard Business Review*. Hbr.org. May 6, 2019. https://hbr.org/2019/05/all-the-ways-hiring-algorithms-can-introduce-bias

20. Ibid, p. 17.

21. Wujciak, M. "4 Companies Using Machine Learning to Keep a Close Eye on Employees." Customer Contact Week. October 18, 2019. https://www.customercontactweekdigital.com/tools-technologies/articles/4-companies-using-machine-learning-to-keep-a-close-eye-on-employees

22. Ibid.

23. Chen, T. "Three Hours of Work a Day? You're Not Fooling Anyone." *The Wall Street Journal*. July 19, 2019. https://www.wsj.com/articles/three-hours-of-work-a-day-youre-not-fooling-anyone-11563528611?mod=djemwhatsnews

24. Falk, W. Editor's Letter. Pressreader.com. February 21, 2020. https://www.pressreader.com/usa/the-week-us/20200221/281547997898431

25. Roose, K. "A Machine May Not Take Your Job, But One Could Become Your Boss." *New York Times*. June 23, 2019. https://www.nytimes.com/2019/06/23/technology/artificial-intelligence-ai-workplace.html

26. Interview with the author May 26, 2020.

27. Barker I. "Technology Is Changing the Way We Work." BetaNews.com. August 23, 2018. https://betanews.com/2018/08/23/technology-changing-workplace/

28. Ibid.

29. Dapcevich, M. "A Terrifying Glimpse at What Office Workers Could Look Like in 20 Years." Iflscience.com. October 28, 2019, 2020. https://www.iflscience.com/health-and-medicine/a-terrifying-glimpse-at-what-office-workers-could-look-like-in-20-years/

30. Ibid.

31. "Will You Lose Your Job to a Robot?" *The Week*. September 22, 2019. https://theweek.com/articles/866339/lose-job-robot

32. Saffron, Inga. "Robots Don't Get Sick": Coronavirus Could Accelerate Automation and Hurt Philly's Low-Wage Workers. *The Philadelphia Inquirer*. July 2, 2020. https://www.inquirer.com/real-estate/inga-saffron /coronavirus-economy-impact-automation-whole-food-philadelphia-20200702.html?utm_medium=referral&utm_source=ios&utm_campaign=app_ios_article&utm_content=KEZRWHTM7JAGJNO5R LWIMNKTBE

33. Hegewisch, Ariane, Chandra Childers, and Heidi Hartmann. *Women, Automation, and the Future of Work*. (Washington, DC: Institute for Women's Policy Research, 2019), p. 16.

34. Ibid.

35. Fox, K., and J. O'Connor. "Five Ways Work Will Change in the Future." *The Guardian*. November 29, 2015. https://www.theguardian .com/society/2015/nov/29/five-ways-work-will-change-future-of-workplace-ai-cloud-retirement-remote

36. Ibid.

37. Ibid.

38. Ibid., p. 6.

39. Ibid.

40. DiStefano, J. "Machine Learning Is the Path to More Sanity in Marketing: JPMorgan Picks AI to Write Ads." *The Philadelphia Inquirer*. July 30, 2019. https://www.inquirer.com/business/phillydeals/jpmorgan-artificial-intelligence-copy-writing-persado-ads-20190730.html

41. "Technological Singularity." *Wikipedia*. August 31, 2020. https://en .wikipedia.org/wiki/Technological_singularity

42. Ibid, p. 6.

43. Sigal, S. "Everywhere Basic Income Has Been Tried in One Map." Vox .com. February 19, 2020. https://www.vox.com/future-perfect/2020/ 2/19/21112570/universal-basic-income-ubi-map

44. Konish, L. "This City Is Giving Residents $500 Per Month. Some Hope It Can Become a National Plan." CNBC. July 12, 2020. https://www.cnbc.com/2020/07/12/coronavirus-relief-stockton-ca-gives-residents-500-per-month.html

45. Matthews, D. "A Guaranteed Income for Every American Would Eliminate Poverty—and It Wouldn't Destroy the Economy." Vox.com. July 23, 2014. https://www.vox.com/2014/7/23/5925041/guaranteed-income-basic-poverty-gobry-labor-supply

46. Zeballos-Roig, J. "The US Is Helping People After They've Lost Their Jobs in the Coronavirus Pandemic. Here's How European Countries Are Helping Workers Keep Them Instead." Markets Insider.com. March 25, 2020. https://markets.businessinsider.com/news/stocks/europe-fight-coronavirus-pay-workers-wages-plan-economy-stay-home-2020-3-1029031212

47. Tyko, K. "Victory for Disability Advocates: Supreme Court Won't Hear Domino's Pizza Accessibility Case." *USA Today*. October 7, 2019. https://www.usatoday.com/story/money/2019/10/07/dominos-pizza-website-accessibility-supreme-court-wont-hear-case/3904582002/

48. Binney, E. "Leadership in the Age of Automation." Society for Human Resources Management. June 18, 2019. https://www.shrm.org/ResourcesAndTools/hr-topics/technology/Pages/Redefining-Leadership-in-the-Age-of-Automation.aspx?utm_source=Editorial%20Newsletters˜NL%202019-6-19%20HR%20Daily&utm_medium=email&utm_campaign=HR%20Daily&mkt_tok=eyJpIjoiWmppCbVptVTBPVGxrWVRNMyIsInQiOiJ5MEl5d2F2SklZWXVnMnVlY1pEeFpFNFwvOGF0ckZWenhUQStvcStWbms5YlFoalhmVzU4U09LREFFFSFo5a3VxZnU2U1lnTVwvUk5yMVdcLzh4WENEEcWVtT2xxbjREZmJwR0RPMDJKbStJcmp1WFZOTmtZNEhQa0IrKzM0VW9hc1hWSCCJ9

49. Davenport, T., and J. Kirby. "Beyond Automation." *Harvard Business Review*. June 2015. https://hbr.org/2015/06/beyond-automation

50. Ibid.

51. Kim, T. "The Gig Economy Is Coming for Your Job." *New York Times*. January 10, 2020. https://www.nytimes.com/2020/01/10/opinion/ sunday/gig-economy-unemployment-automation.html

52. Bughin, Jacques, Susan Lund, and Jaana Remes. "Rethinking Work in the Digital Age." McKinsey.Com. October 24, 2016. https:// www.mckinsey.com/business-functions/organization/our-insights/ rethinking-work-in-the-digital-age#

53. Campbell, B. "AFL-CIO 2nd-in-Command Discusses Labor's 'Next Frontier.'" Law 360. January 17, 2020. https://www.law360.com/ employment/articles/1235233?utm_source=shared-articles&utm_ medium=email&utm_campaign=shared-articles

Chapter 6   The Education We Need Is Changing

1. Mintz, S. "Why Education Will Change." Inside Higher Ed. October 3, 2019. https://www.insidehighered.com/blogs/higher-ed-gamma/ why-higher-education-will-change

2. "What Is a Trade School?" The Best Schools. August 11, 2020. https:// thebestschools.org/magazine/trade-schools-rise-ashes-college-degree/

3. Ibid.

4. Grawe. N. "Americans Are Having Fewer Kids. What Will that Mean for Higher Education?" Hbr.org. October 17, 2019. https://hbr.org/ 2019/10/americans-are-having-fewer-kids-what-will-that-mean-for- higher-education

5. Howard, J. "Coronavirus Pandemic Could Lead to Up to 500,000 Fewer US Births, Study Suggests." CNN. June 23, 2020. https://www .cnn.com/2020/06/23/health/coronavirus-birth-rate-brookings-study- wellness/index.html

6. Ibid.

7. Hufford, A. "American Factories Demand White-Collar Education for Blue-Collar Work." *Wall Street Journal.* December 9, 2019. https://www.wsj.com/articles/american-factories-demand-white-collar-education-for-blue-collar-work-11575907185

8. Ibid.

9. "Phlebotomy Technician Training." MiraCosta College. February 16, 2020. http://tci.miracosta.edu/courses-health-phlebotomy.html

10. Sánchez, N. "Community Colleges and the Future of Workforce Development." *Forbes.* October 24, 2019. https://www.forbes.com/sites/nancyleesanchez/2019/10/24/community-colleges-and-the-future-of-workforce-development/#4f0e79dc681f

11. "Cal Poly Learn by Doing." Cal Poly Technic University. June 16, 2020. https://www.calpoly.edu/learn-by-doing

12. "How I Learn by Doing: Pashion Project." CalPoly. July 2, 2020. https://magazine.calpoly.edu/fall-2017/pashion-project/

13. Tech Blog. Diamandis. July 2, 2020. https://www.diamandis.com/blog/future-of-higher-education-apprenticeships

14. Ibid.

15. "What Is Trade School?"

16. Ibid.

17. "Seventy-Percent of Contractors Have a Hard Time Finding Qualified Craft Workers to Hire Amid Growing Construction Demand, National Survey Finds." Association of General Contractors. August 29, 2017. https://www.agc.org/news/2017/08/29/seventy-percent-contractors-have-hard-time-finding-qualified-craft-workers-hire-am-0

18. "Advancing CTE in State and Local Career Pathways." Cte.ed.gov. June 16, 2020. https://cte.ed.gov/initiatives/advancing-cte-in-state-and-local-career-pathways-system

19. "The Good Jobs Project." Good Jobs Data. June 16, 2020. https://goodjobsdata.org/

20. Farrer, L. "Future of Education and Future of Work—Do They Match? *Forbes*. April 30, 2019. https://www.forbes.com/sites/laurelfarrer/2019/04/30/future-of-education-and-future-of-work-do-they-match/#3a3bd2b879f0

21. Ferguson, A. "The College President Who Simply Won't Raise Tuition." *The Atlantic*. April 2020. https://www.theatlantic.com/magazine/archive/2020/04/mitch-daniels-purdue/606772/

22. Weller, C. "5 People from Around the World Share What It's Like to Get Free College Education." *Business Insider*. December 1, 2017. https://www.businessinsider.com/free-college-education-what-its-like-2017-10

23. Bridgeland, John, and John J. Dilulio. "Will America Embrace National Service?" October 10, 2019. The Brookings Institution.

24. Decety, J., and W. Ickes. *The Social Neuroscience of Empathy* (Cambridge, MA: MIT Press, 2011).

25. "African Americans and the GI Bill." *Wikipedia*. June 24, 2020. https://en.wikipedia.org/wiki/African_Americans_and_the_G.I._Bill#:~:text=Bill.,as%20much%20as%20White%20Americans

26. "The Economic Value of National Service." Voices for Service. July 2, 2020. https://voicesforservice.org/research-and-reports/economic-value-national-service/

27. Ibid.

28. "Will America Embrace National Service?", p. 25.

29. Ibid.

30. "Mandatory National Service—Top 3 Pros and Cons." Procon.org. April 25, 2019. https://www.procon.org/headlines/mandatory-national-service-top-3-pros-and-cons/

31. Yaw, G. "To Unite Us, America Should Require Mandatory Service." Penn Live. January 30, 2019. https://www.pennlive.com/opinion/2018/04/to_unite_us_america_should_req.html

32. Mintz, S. "Why Higher Ed Will Change." Inside Higher Ed. October 3, 2019. https://www.insidehighered.com/blogs/higher-ed-gamma/why-higher-education-will-change

33. Marcus, J. "How Technology Is Changing the Future of Higher Education." *New York Times*. February 20, 2020. https://www.nytimes.com/2020/02/20/education/learning/education-technology.html

34. Cheng, M. "Howt Universities Are Starting to Prepare Students for the Gig Economy." QZ.com. October 17, 2019. https://qz.com/work/1724712/how-universities-are-preparing-students-for-the-gig-economy/

35. Ibid.

Chapter 7 The Climate Is Changing

1. "Climate Change: How Do We Know?" NASA. July 15, 2020. https://climate.nasa.gov/evidence/

2. Ibid.

3. Ruggeri, A. "How Climate Change Will Transform Business and the Workforce." BBC. July 9, 2017.

4. Harper, K. "6 Ways Climate Change and Disease Helped Topple the Roman Empire." Vox.com. October 30, 2017. https://www.vox.com/the-big-idea/2017/10/30/16568716/six-ways-climate-change-disease-toppled-roman-empire

5. "A Student's Guide to Global Climate Change." Environmental Protection Agency. August 18, 2020. https://archive.epa.gov/climatechange/kids/scientists/proof.html

6. "Greenhouse Effect." *National Geographic*. August 18, 2020. https://www.nationalgeographic.org/encyclopedia/greenhouse-effect/

7. Kaplan, S., and E. Guskin. "Most American Teens Are Frightened by Climate Change, Poll Finds, and About 1 in 4 Are Taking Action." *The Washington Post*. September 15, 2019. https://www.washingtonpost.com/science/most-american-teens-are-frightened-by-climate-

change-poll-finds-and-about-1-in-4-are-taking-action/2019/09/15/
1936da1c-d639-11e9-9610-fb56c5522e1c_story.html

8. Irfin, U. "Why the US Bears the Most Responsibility for Climate
   Chane, in One Chart." Vox.com. December 4, 2019. https://www.vox
   .com/energy-and-environment/2019/4/24/18512804/climate-change-
   united-states-china-emissions#:~:text=And%20since%20that%20time
   %2C%20some,more%20carbon%20dioxide%20than%20others.&
   text=What's%20abundantly%20clear%20is%20that,gas%20emitter
   %20on%20the%20planet.&text=China%20now%20emits%20more
   %20than,India's%20emissions%20are%20rapidly%20rising

9. Ridge, T. "My Fellow Conservatives Are Out of Touch on the Environment." *The Atlantic*. April 22, 2020. https://www.theatlantic.com/
   ideas/archive/2020/04/environment-gop-out-touch/610333/

10. Freedman, A., and C. Mooney. "Major New Study Rules Out Less
    Severe Global Warming Scenarios." *The Washington Post*. July 22,
    2020. https://www.washingtonpost.com/weather/2020/07/22/climate-
    sensitivity-co2/

11. "The Economic Risks of Climate Change in the United States." Risky
    Business. August 16, 2020. http://riskybusiness.org/report/national/

12. Marsh, Kaufman, et al. "Here's How Climate Change Will Impact the
    U.S." CNN.com. November 27, 2018. https://www.cnn.com/2018/
    11/27/health/climate-change-impact-by-region/index.html

13. "The Economic Risks of Climate Change in the United States."

14. Kahn, D., and C. Bermel. "California Has First Rolling Blackouts
    in 19 Years and Everyone Faces Blame." Politico.com. August 18,
    2020. https://www.politico.com/states/california/story/2020/08/18/
    california-has-first-rolling-blackouts-in-19-years-and-everyone-faces-
    blame-1309757

15. Ibid.

16. Ibid.

17. "Climate Change and Human Health." World Health Organization. August 16, 2020. https://www.who.int/globalchange/climate/summary/en/index5.html

18. Ibid.

19. Bouma, M., and H. van der Kaay. "The El Niño Southern Oscillation and the Historic Malaria Epidemics on the Indian Subcontinent and Sri Lanka: An Early Warning System for Future Epidemics?" *Tropical Medicine and International Health* Vol. 1, No. 1 (1996): 86–96.

20. Yong, E. "How the Pandemic Defeated America." *The Atlantic*. September 2020. https://www.theatlantic.com/magazine/archive/2020/09/coronavirus-american-failure/614191/

21. Davenport, C. "Industry Awakens to Threat of Climate Change." *New York Times*. January 24, 2014. https://www.nytimes.com/2014/01/24/science/earth/threat-to-bottom-line-spurs-action-on-climate.html?_r=2

22. Ibid.

23. "How Climate Change Will Transform Business and the Workforce."

24. Ibid.

25. "Three Quarters of Millennials Would Take a Pay Cut to Work for a Socially Responsible Company, According to Research from Cone Communications." PRNewswire. November 2,, 2016. https://www.prnewswire.com/news-releases/three-quarters-of-millennials-would-take-a-pay-cut-to-work-for-a-socially-responsible-company-according-to-research-from-cone-communications-300355311.html

26. "Environmental, Social, and Governance (ESG) Criteria." *Investopedia*. September 3, 2020. https://www.investopedia.com/terms/e/environmental-social-and-governance-esg-criteria.asp

27. Marshall, E. "Goldman Sachs Says It Will Support 'Green' Initiatives More Forcefully." Reuters. December 16, 2019. https://www.reuters.com/article/us-goldman-sachs-environment/goldman-sachs-says-it-will-support-green-initiatives-more-forcefully-idUSKBN1YK1U6

28. "The Economic Risks of Climate Change in the United States."

29. "Question: What Does the Public Think About Climate Change and Carbon Pricing?" Citizens Climate Lobby. July 23, 2020. https://citizensclimatelobby.org/laser-talks/polling-data/

30. "The Tax Burden on Tobacco, 2017." *Youth Risk Behavior Survey, 2017* (Washington, DC: CDC, Bureau of Labor Statistics).

31. "Making Wine in a Changing Climate." International Wineries for Climate Change. WebEx presentation. July 23, 2020. https://laffortusa.webex.com/recordingservice/sites/laffortusa/recording/play/8201accf32ef463bb0cb5881ada52770

32. Kummer, F. "New Jersey to Build Massive $400M 'Wind Port,' Gov. Murphy Says." *The Philadelphia Inquirer*. June 16, 2020. https://www.inquirer.com/science/climate/new-jersey-murphy-wind-port-power-20200616.html?utm_medium=referral&utm_source=ios&utm_campaign=app_ios_article&utm_content=ENK7OTHJPRAM5KYK2VERY2DKMI

33. "Top Companies Urge White House to Stay in the Paris Agreement." Center for Climate and Energy Solutions. July 23, 2020. https://www.c2es.org/press-release/major-companies-urge-white-house-to-stay-in-paris-agreement/

34. Telephone call with the author, July 17, 2020.

35. "Assessing the Impact of a Carbon Tax from a Business Perspective." IT Industry. July 23, 2020. https://drive.google.com/file/d/1Y0aJbeutB9TbCIhCc1skd-0g0CNck2U_/view

36. Ibid.

37. "Green New Deal." *Wikipedia*. July 22, 2020. https://en.wikipedia.org/wiki/Green_New_Deal

38. Kelly, A. "Even Oil Companies Want a Federal Price on Carbon." WBUR.org. June 19, 2019. https://www.wbur.org/cognoscenti/2019/06/19/corporate-america-wants-a-price-on-carbon-ceres-anne-kelly

39. Ibid.

40. Ibid.

41. Siegner, C. "Danone, Mars, Nestle and Unilever Launch Sustainable Food Policy Alliance." FoodDive.com. July 23, 2020. https://www .fooddive.com/news/danone-mars-nestle-and-unilever-launch-sustainable-food-policy-alliance/527699/

42. "Laffort Webinar: Making Wine in a Changing Climate." BCLResources.org. July 22, 2020. https://sites.google.com/view/ bcl-resources/home/industry/food-beverage/winery/laffort-webinar? authuser=0

43. Ibid.

44. "The U.S. Business Case for a Carbon Fee and Dividend: How Small and Medium-Sized Enterprises Will be Affected." Business Climate Leaders. March 2019. https://static1.squarespace.com/ static/588eb46a579fb35be4fd8d67/t/5d045b0bbc404e000101b076/ 1560566540515/BCL.2019.HOW.CFD.AFFECTS.SMEs.6.14.pdf

45. Lombrana, L., and H. Warren. "A Pandemic That Cleared Skies and Halted Cities Isn't Slowing Global Warming." Bloomberg.com May 8, 2020. https://www.bloomberg.com/graphics/2020-how-coronavirus-impacts-climate-change/

46. Kaur, H. "The Coronavirus Pandemic Is Making Earth Vibrate Less." CNN. April 4, 2020. https://www.cnn.com/2020/04/02/world/ coronavirus-earth-seismic-noise-scn-trnd/index.html

47. Frost, N. "A Decade Ago, the US as Promised High Speed Rail—So Where Is It?" QZ.com December 27, 2019. https://qz.com/1761495/ this-is-why-the-us-still-doesnt-have-high-speed-trains/

Conclusion

1. "About B Corps." Bcroporation.net. September 3, 2020. https:// bcorporation.net/about-b-corps

2. Ibid.

INDEX

9/11, impact, 3

A

AB5. *See* California
Active listening skills,
    importance, 3
Advantage Convey, 128
Affirmative action, quotas
    (contrast), 61–62
Affordable Care Act (ACA),
    89–90
AFL-CIO, 121
  formation, 34
Alaska Permanent Fund, citizen
    payments, 116
Amazon, AI tracking, 108–109
America
  annual household income
    (1905), 29
  demographic change, 64–66
  flex, importance, 167–169
  foundation, change
    (importance), 23
  industrial output, decline, 33
  industry, flex, 163–164
  political schism, 6
  safety/security, shift, 3

  socioeconomic mobility,
    limitation, 85
  survival. *See* Preindustrial
    America.
  workforce, minority workers
    (entry), 64–65
American Association of Retired
    Persons (AARP),
    supplemental coverage, 87
American Dream, 23
  disappearance, 8
  veterans usage, 138–139
American Recovery and
    Reinvestment Act (2010,
    168–169
Americans with Disabilities Act
    (ADA), compliance, 118
American System, 26–27
America Online (AOL), 155
AmeriCorps, 140
  education award, 142
  funding, 139
Antidiscrimination/
    antiharassment policies,
    enforcement, 83
Apartheid, existence, 37
Applications (apps), usage,
    101–102